Breaking The Chains
From Worship To

Warfare

Revised Edition

Breaking The Chains
From Worship To
Warfare

MATTIE NOTTAGE
MINISTRIES
INTERNATIONAL

"Surviving The Conflict"
DR. MATTIE M. NOTTAGE

Breaking The Chains, From Worship To Warfare
By Mattie M. Nottage

Mattie Nottage Ministries, International
P.O. Box SB–52524
Nassau, N. P. Bahamas
Tel: (888) 825-7568 or (242) 698-1383
www.mattienottage.org

First printed in the United States of America by Xulon Press
ISBN-13: 978-1-60034-788-7
ISBN-10: 1-60034-788-6

Revised edition printed in the United States of America
Mattie Nottage Ministries, International
ISBN-13: 978-0-615-35740-9

Book cover designed by: Vision Media Bahamas
Edited by: Beyond All Barriers Publications & Media Group
Format and Interior design by: Beyond All Barriers Publications & Media Group

DEDICATION

This book is dedicated to God my Father and the blessed Holy Spirit, who taught me how to worship and dance before Him as a Princess and to leave His presence empowered as a Warrior. God Himself is a Man of war, Jehovah is His name and at the same time He is the lover of all worship offered to Him in spirit and in truth. This is for my God who has called me to the kingdom for such a time as this.

To my best friend, spiritual covering, husband and Pastor, Apostle Edison Nottage, thank you for your strength and support. I love you!

And finally to my three children and adopted daughter who are "warriors in waiting", thank you for your motivation. I love you all!

ACKNOWLEDGEMENT

First of all, I acknowledge God the Father, Son and Holy Spirit whose inspiration led me to write this book to empower and equip believers, everywhere. I count it an honor to be a servant and vessel of His.

To the family of Believers Faith Outreach Ministries in Nassau, Bahamas Believers Faith Breakthrough Ministries in south Florida and the friends and partners of Mattie Nottage Ministries International, thank you. Your prayers have lifted me on angels' and eagles' wings.

PROPHETIC FOREWORD

Seated around what has been transformed as the "Table of Birthing and Revelation", Prophetess Mattie pours out the fountain of divinely inspired revelations and utterances impressed upon her by the Holy Spirit. Very late one Thursday night, on August 24th, 2006, God spoke this prophetic utterance through her.

"The church is in a season of major transition from a church mindset to a kingdom dimension. The impending move of God is coming forth with a rushing mighty wind. With this paradigm shift, the move will be predicated by the prophets' ability to release a sound in the earth realm such that was never experienced before, but similar to that in the days of Adam, Ezekiel and on the Day of Pentecost.

The Ark of God shall return to the people of God so that the earth will "ring" (live) again as in *1 Samuel 4:5*. The coming move of God is going to shake the very foundation of the established Christian church and the world at large.

Everything, saith the Lord, that is parched and dry shall begin to live again. Revelation, wisdom, and knowledge shall be increased like never before. God shall raise up an army from the four corners of the earth, of young people and children, men and women who have not bowed themselves to idols nor defiled the altars of God.

No longer will we, the kingdom citizens, be divided in our faith, but in a spirit of unity and oneness, begin to manifest and show forth the supernatural power of God. The blind will see, the deaf will hear and those that were once obscured and laughed at will be brought to the forefront. He will judge His bride and cleanse her from all filthiness of the flesh and of the spirit, presenting her to Himself glorified, not having spot or wrinkle." *Selah*

PREFACE
"Dance of a Warrior-Princess"

In this hour, God is seeking to raise up a prophetic people who are not ashamed or afraid to come before Him and dance in worship. Even as the Psalmist David danced before the Lord with all of his might until his outer garments fell off, God is requiring His people to unashamedly elevate to a level of passionate, soulful worship with boldness. He is seeking those who would be willing to demonstrate their love for Him, even in the presence of others; those who are prepared to lay down their pride, title, socio-economic status and position in this life, to "dance" in His presence.

Over the years, the Spirit of God has released an anointing upon my life in the area of breakthrough and deliverance. Week after week, God has graced me to pour into the lives of His people. Many can bear witness to the transformation that has taken place in their lives, I believe because of my yieldedness to the Spirit of God.

I have seen many people who were brought to their knees, not in humiliation or shame, but in humble brokenness before the King of kings and the Lord of lords asking, "What must I do to be saved?"

Then, amazingly, one Sunday morning, an unusual transformation took place, not only in the lives of the people to whom I ministered, but in my very own life.

For a moment, I replaced my three-inch St. John's pumps for ballerina shoes; my preaching robes for peasant skirts and overlays and transformed, but for a moment, what has been called my *"fire pulpit"* into a palace; and danced before the Lord.

As the music filled the atmosphere and I began to dance, I soon forgot that there were other people in the room. In that moment, all I saw was my King and my only prayer was that I would please Him with my worship dance offering. I could not hear the audience and many dare not even breathe so as not to interrupt this artistic expression of worship that I offered to God.

It was a dance that broke through the barriers of fear, the flesh and pride. A dance that propelled and compelled everyone who experienced it, to come out of the small box that circumstance, life, people and even their own fears had placed them in. A dance that said, "You can do it!" You can do all that God is calling you to do.

It does not mean that you won't be afraid. "Do it anyway!" It does not mean that you won't get anxious. "Do it anyway!" It does not mean that you won't need someone to encourage you along the way. "Do it anyway! You can do it!" *"You can dance!* Nothing can stop you, except you!"

Later, many people gave God glory and said how blessed they were by the entire worship experience. Others became broken and said that without uttering a word, I had preached one of my most powerful and compelling messages.

Within the prophetic symbolisms of the dramatic expression of intimacy and adoration in dance, they began to see the power every believer possessed in worshipping God. That if you would humble yourself to give God all the worship and glory He deserves, there is nothing that can stop or limit you from doing what He has placed inside of you to do. Once the alabaster box of your life is broken, the fragrance of the anointing that God has placed within you will overwhelm everything and everyone around you.

With the meticulous creativity and assistance of the Holy Spirit, set your own stage and then dance before the King of kings and Lord of lords. *Dance!* And know that your dance is not for anyone else's applause. *He is calling for a private audience with you. So dance before the Lord!*

TABLE OF CONTENTS

PART I

WORSHIP

CHAPTER ONE

TRUE WORSHIP OR SPIRITUAL HARLOTRY

FROM WORSHIP TO WARFARE

It is believed that of the over seventy percent (70%) of people who attend church, that only 30% of them have actually been born again and understand what it truly means to worship God. You can decide to either live a lifestyle of true worship or decide to indulge in the practice of spiritual harlotry.

Over a decade ago, everywhere you turned, people were embracing the concept of worship. Even in various traditional settings the word *worship* has become synonymous with melodious song services and hymns.

Although the corporate worship experience is somewhat misunderstood, people had a basic idea that they wanted to do something more than just sing. People realized that they wanted more than just a good time or a jump up and down roller coaster ride – they wanted a real worship encounter with the Spirit of God.

Worship

Worship is the releasing of the inner intimate expression of one's being to God. His creation of man in His own image made man the very expression of His divine will. Man's primary responsibility is to serve God in spirit and in truth. Our fully submitted will to that of the Creator would bring forth profound glory, which is all the excellencies of God revealed in our lives, homes, marriages, churches, businesses, and more.

God's breath into Adam tied him eternally to Himself. Adam had authority over the entire earth domain and operated in a realm with God that was so powerful that it positioned him to be fruitful, multiply, replenish and subdue the earth, all at the same time. Everything that a man could ever want, he had. He had access to and intimacy with God, but he lost this because of disobedience. Sin had eternally separated him from this easy access into the presence of God.

Jesus' death, burial and resurrection became the open door for each one of us to now enter. Even as the veil in the temple was ripped from top to bottom, so was Jesus' flesh, in order to give us entrance to the throne through worship. In *Isaiah 1:18 it says, "Come now, and let us reason together, says the Lord..."*

Hebrews 4:16 says, "Let us therefore come boldly unto the throne of grace, that we may obtain mercy, and find grace to help in time of need."

2

Our acceptance of Jesus as Lord and Saviour automatically opens the door for us to enter the presence of our God and King. The first Garden of Eden no longer exists but the eternal Eden is right where you are. Elohim, the Creator of the Universe is no longer just in a garden nor in tents made with hands, but He wants to have divine communion and habitation with His prized creation; He desires to "Tabernacle" with man.

"What is man, that thou art mindful of him? and the son of man, that thou visitest him?" (Psalm 8:4)

When people do not believe or see God as Elohim, The Creator of all things, they will not worship Him as such. If they place their confidence in Mary, Buddah or even their own self they will not worship God. Jehovah, God is the ultimate King and, by design, He has an established domain. God's domain or His kingdom is where His rulership is established or where His way of doing things is in effect. His ultimate desire is to see everything functioning in earth, as it is being done in Heaven.

Worshipping God is the key which gives you access to every benefit in the kingdom of God. Worship is a lifestyle. It is when you seek to please God, every moment of your life. Worship is more than just serving but involves giving oneself wholly to God and fulfilling His divine will.

Your level of worship is based on your understanding of who God truly is by the revelation of the Holy Spirit. In **Hebrews 11:6** the Word of God says that when we come to God we must first believe that He exists and that He is a Rewarder of them that diligently seek Him. Therefore, true worship is based on your faith and willingness to acknowledge and know God.

In *Revelation 1:6* it also declares that "we are kings" and as kings we have been given a domain, which is the earth. In *Genesis 1:26-28* it shows that God created man and gave him *dominion* over everything that He had created. Man's God-given assignment was to dominate, subdue, replenish and multiply all things on the earth. So the earth is the domain, sphere or region that God has given us to rule over.

Man's ultimate purpose is to fulfill the will and purpose of God. The only way that we can even know the will of God and accomplish it is when we worship Him. When we offer worship to God, we build a relationship with Him that empowers us to fulfill God's divine purpose in everything that we can see, hear or do in the earth; even as it is being done in heaven. That which is impossible in Man's strength becomes possible when he begins to worship God.

Everything that you will ever desire or seek to accomplish in life is wrapped up in your worship. Your worship is the pre-requisite to your miracle.

Warfare

Warfare, in my opinion, is defined a hostile battle between rivals or enemies. Warfare is normally engaged because there is something of great value at stake. The Greek word for warfare, which is *"strateia" (pronounced strat-i-ah)* suggests military service and strategic military engagement. In the realm of the spirit it denotes an apostolic mandate to fight. God has released upon you an apostolic anointing to fight and win in spiritual warfare; if only to protect what He has already given you.

At the turn of the 21st century, the word "warfare" became more and more prevalent in both the secular and

Christian circles. There was, and still is, the war on drugs, war on domestic violence and child abuse, chemical and biological wars, and mo.

On September 11, 2001, there was an unthinkable, unimaginable attack waged by terrorists that hit America, killing nearly 3,000 people. Today, the war on terrorism is still a primary focus of the United States Government. The word of God says that, *"... in the last days perilous times shall come." (2 Timothy 3:1) "And ye shall hear of wars and rumors of wars..." (Matthew 24:6)*

The leaders of these terrorist groups have set out on a mission to incite fear and panic in the minds and hearts of every American and the world at large. Their hatred and anger for Jews and even Christians, fuel their diabolical plans to kill and destroy even the innocent. God, through His word, admonishes us to not be afraid.

"... Thou shall not be afraid of the terror by night... Nor for the pestilence that walketh in darkness; nor for the destruction that wasteth at noonday." (Psalm 91:5 - 6)

The Counterattack

When engaged in a war, leaders of countries strategically plan a counterattack against their enemy. They immediately rally their secret information services, their allies, their military reinforcements and other sources to ascertain what weapons their enemies have and how they plan to use them. Any successful war strategist makes immediate preparation to launch their armed forces to disarm and dismantle the enemy by whatever means necessary.

When attacked by terrorists, the Government of The United States of America launched a relentless counterattack and converted its entire nation into warriors or at least to think like warriors.

Similarly, God is now seeking to transform His children from living passive defeated lives into that of victorious, militant warriors, who know how to wage strategic warfare and are able to counterattack the tactics and stratagem of the enemy.

According to Genesis 3:5, the enemy has sought to consistently attack the lives of believers since time began.

"And I will put enmity between thee and the woman, and between thy seed and her seed; it shall bruise thy head, and thou shalt bruise his heel"

During these attacks, many believers have sat passively by and watched the enemy wreak havoc in their lives. Loved ones have succumbed to lifestyles of alcohol and drugs, children have "run wild" and dangerously out of control, "strange" women have captured the minds and attention of once faithful husbands. In the midst of these attacks many believers have become complacent, not doing anything to remedy their vexing problems. This must change. You must rise up and fight.

"There hath no temptation taken you but such as is common to man: but God is faithful, who will not suffer you to be tempted above that ye are able; but will with the temptation also make a way to escape, that ye may be able to bear it."
(1 Corinthians 10:13)

SPIRITUAL HARLOTRY AND THE SPIRIT OF WHOREDOM

From the very beginning of time God had created man to give Him praise and worship. In *Isaiah 43:7*, God clearly states His divine purpose for creating man,

> *"...for I (God) have created him (man) for my glory..."*

Praise is an aspect of worship where we audibly and verbally express our thanks and appreciation unto God. For the most part, it is for what He has done and can be accompanied by clapping or lifting up our hands. Furthermore, praise emphasizes the acts of God or the works of God and can also be used in warfare as a powerful weapon against the enemy.

Worship, on the other hand, shows our humble adoration for who God is, what He means to us and is displayed by humbly bowing and totally surrender ourselves to Him. In the Hebrew, worship was looked at as involving our entire life, in that, everything we do in servitude to God, should give profound glory, honor and majesty to Him. In the Hebrew this is called *abodah (pronounced ab-o-daw)* and is translated as servitude, service, ministry, etc.

Worship is also consecrating a specific time for the glorification and adoration of God. This involves prostrating and bowing before God and giving ourselves wholly to Him. In Hebrew this is called *shachah (pronounced shaw-khaw).* However, it is when we begin to deviate from this, to worship and serve other gods, that we are practicing what is called *spiritual harlotry.*

"My people ask counsel at their stocks, and their staff declareth unto them: for the spirit of whoredoms hath caused them to err, and they have gone awhoring from under their God." (Hosea 4:12)

Spiritual Harlotry is a form of spiritual adultery which occurs when the people of God seek to serve other gods or place any idol before the One True God. We must be very careful in this hour, not to become guilty of spiritual whoredom. In the book of Deuteronomy, the Word of God reveals that Israel had gone "awhoring" after other gods. Upon bringing them out of Egypt and into Canaan, God had warned them against the sins of idolatry and spiritual adultery.

"And it shall be, if thou do at all forget the Lord thy God, and walk after other gods, and serve them, and worship them, I testify against you this day that ye shall surely perish."
(Deuteronomy 8:19)

In fact, He told them that when they entered Canaan the first thing He needed them to do was to break down all the altars, false idols and to burn down their groves *(Exodus 34:13)*. The Canaanites worshipped Baal and, as their Egyptian counterparts, anything that benefited them, including the sun, moon and stars.

SPIRITUAL KINGDOM IDOLATRY

God made it clear in Exodus 20 that we should have no other gods besides Him. He defines Himself as a jealous God. In other words, He does not seek to share His Lordship with any other. Many of you may be guilty of having placed something in your life before God, whether it was your favorite television program, a movie star, your career, families, homes, cars or other material gain, somehow it kept you from the presence of God.

The children of Israel had totally forgotten about the God who had brought them out of the land of bondage and they began worshipping idols of gold, brass and silver. Many of them were bitten by fiery serpents and died in the wilderness never making it to the Promised Land. "You must never forget the God who brought you out." *(Deuteronomy 8)*

Everybody's Egypt and Pharaoh may be different, but I am sure that we can all testify of how God delivered us out of something that had us in slavery or bondage.

"SPIRITUAL WHOREDOM CAUSES DISLOYALTY"

Having two lovers brews contention, frustration and competition. It is extremely difficult to truly be in love with so many people at once and be faithful to all. Someone will be robbed or short-changed; normally it is the "piggy in the middle".

"No man can serve two masters: for either he will hate the one, and love the other; or else he will hold to the one, and despise the other."
(Matthew 6:24a)

Jesus further said, "If any man will come after me let him deny himself, and take up his cross and follow me." (Matthew 16:24)

"SELF DENIAL IS A MUST!"

Paul said, *"No man that warreth entangles
himself with the affairs of this life; ..."*
(2 Timothy 2:4)

In other words, *"You cannot serve God and
mammon." (Matthew 6:24b)*

People always want all the benefits from God but only
call on Him when they have a flat tire, no money in the bank,
or their marriage is on the rocks. God is not looking for a *"one
night stand."* He is looking for a life-long relationship. It is
my prayer that every believer will come into this personal
relationship with Him.

It is important to understand that it is the enemy's
ultimate plan to keep mankind in bondage and devoid of this
personal relationship with God. His subtle strategy is to keep
people so wrapped up and entangled in worldly, ungodly
systems that we are not able to focus on truly understanding
who God is.

If many of you will be honest, had you not been so
worried about paying your mortgage, sending your children
off to college, paying your credit card bill, or trying to keep
up with the latest fashion trend, or what was happening in
the life of your favorite Hollywood star, you would be able to
spend more time in the presence of God. However, the
enemy has cleverly devised many systems to prevent this.
One such system is the system of Babylon.

Babylon

Babylon was originally called Babel, which meant
"confusion." It was an old Mesopotamian city founded by
Nimrod around 747 BC. This ancient empire was directly
influenced by three other cultures which are the Arabs,

Chaldeans and Assyrians but later developed its own laws, culture, and religious belief system.

After being free from Egypt, the Children of Israel experienced another period of slavery and captivity, this time in Babylon. They were forced to worship false gods or face death. The City of Babylon itself was eventually destroyed, but suffices it to say, its spirit still lives on today.

THE BABYLON SYSTEM

The spirit of Babylon has set up an entire system or order which comprises of several strongholds or is governed by three (3) major systems, including the **political, economical, and religious systems** and is designed to keep the people of God entangled and overly consumed with the world's way of doing things, in ignorance to God's way of doing things, and ultimately oblivious to God Himself.

> 15"*Do not love or cherish the world or the things that are in the world. If anyone loves the world, love for the Father is not in him.*"
> 16"*For all that is in the world – the lust of the flesh [craving for sensual gratification] and the lust of the eyes [greedy longings of the mind] and the pride of life [assurance in one's own resources or in the stability of earthly things] – these do not come from the Father but are from the world [itself].*"
> (1 John 2:15-16AMP)

Politically, the system of Babylon seeks to control individuals through subtle immoral laws and credence. These laws seek to negatively affect the overall well-being of believers and their families, making it difficult to survive the many bureaucracies of the land. A perfect example is recorded in the book of Daniel where King Nebuchadnezzar passed a decree that at the sound of the music everyone should bow to the image. Shadrach, Meshach and Abednego refused to do so and were thrown into the fiery furnace.

The Religious System of Babylon works similarly to its political counterpart in that it institutes basic laws and doctrines which suggest that adherence and obedience to such laws and practices will foster a closer relationship with God. For example, with warm smiles and acceptance it encourages people to join a local church.

However soon after, the implementation of legalistic laws and unscriptural rituals causes these individuals to remain in spiritual bondage and never experience the full measure of God's divine blessings. Therefore it is incumbent upon each believer to seek the face of God and His divine will and purpose for his life. Jesus said in *Colossians 2:8:*

"Beware lest any man spoil you through philosophy and vain deceit, after the tradition of men, after the rudiments of the world, and not after Christ."

Finally, the *Babylonian Economic System* has been fully designed to ensnare and ultimately destroy those who serve it. The currency of Babylon is called *Mammon* or "Economic Idolatry", in our language. As we saw in *Matthew 6:24b,* Jesus told us that we cannot serve God and mammon. In other words, even though we need money, we should not worship or become a slave to it.

In my opinion, the spirit of mammon is not just money but it represents a world system or world view that controls the way money flows. It is a conglomerate of patterns and systems or operations within systems designed to establish negative strongholds in an effort to keep individuals in poverty.

Further, the spirit of mammon goes after the minds of believers convincing them that investing in the kingdom of God is worthless, while investing in other commodities will be fruitful. Satan seeks to pervert the minds of individuals into believing that they can invest their monies into anything else in the world's system, as long as they do not give it to God or His Kingdom.

As a result, many arguments have risen where people tend to challenge the kingdom principle of tithing and giving offerings. Further, many seek to question why believers feel it necessary to give towards the advancement of the Kingdom when it is the system of Babylon that seeks to keep people bound and in bondage to spirits of poverty and lack.

On the other hand, the enemy seeks to cause people to think that because of their wealth, they are self-sufficient and have no need for God.

MONEY ITSELF IS NOT EVIL, BUT IT IS THE LOVE OF MONEY THAT BREWS EVIL.

The world's current economical system has been set up to keep you in bondage to it. For example, a credit card is given to you with a two thousand dollar ($2,000.00) credit limit. Depending on the interest rate, it may take you approximately twenty (20) years to pay back the principal and interest charges if you are only making the minimum payment.

The same concept applies to a home mortgage if you do not pay lump sums towards your principal. You can spend the first several years just paying interest and actually pay back double the amount you initially borrowed.

In our society today, it is easier to get a loan for a vehicle than it is to finance a business. It is very clear, therefore, that God's will for His children is to dominate, subdue, and replenish.

You must now begin to free yourself from the strongholds of these systems by positioning yourselves in a place of spiritual, financial, and physical liberty where you are able to allow God to control your destiny through the power of Jesus Christ.

In order to overcome the pressures dictated by the spirit of Babylon, you must be prepared to:
- to renew your mind
- to seek God concerning His divine will and purpose for your life
- to go after your dreams and vision, knowing that it is God who gives you the power to get wealth

THE SPIRIT OF BABYLON

The spirit of Babylon literally exists in the spirit realm and seeks to control the life and destinies of people, churches, communities and nations at large. It subtly introduces its concepts, principles, and ideologies to those oblivious to its ungodly influences. This system is designed to capture and lock you into its satanic vice grip, ultimately seeking to undermine God's divine plans and purposes.

The spirit of Babylon forms ungodly confederations and alliances. Some of its cohorts are the spirits of Jezebel, Pharaoh, Nebuchadnezzar, Herod, Leviathan, Egypt and

Mammon. These are all evil spirits that work like an underground Mafia to keep you in bondage.

Additionally, the spirit of Babylon is a spirit of deception that seeks to keep you spiritually blind, deaf and dumb to the things of God. It entices you to be more loyal to your job, business, politics, money, cults, forms of culture, music or any other thing, rather than the kingdom of God.

Since we are in a spiritual war, the attacks that the enemy sends are spiritual. These spirits may work through governments, systems, organizations or people. The only way we can get to know God and His ways is if we are willing to break away from these worldly systems and aggressively seek out the presence of God.

> *"And be not conformed to this world: but be ye transformed by the renewing of your mind,..."*
> *(Romans 12:2)*

> *"Love not the world, neither the things that are in the world." (1 John 2:15a)*
> *"For all that is in the world, the lust of the flesh, and the lust of the eyes, and the pride of life,..." (1 John 2:16)*

Some manifestations of the principality spirits *of Jezebel, Herod, Babylon, Pharaoh, Nebuchadnezzar, Egypt, Mammon,* and *Leviathan* in your life, church or country are:

- *Human Secularism*
- *Demasculinization*
- *Moral Decay*
- *Poverty*
- *Racism*
- *Segregation*
- *Victimization*

- *Forced Labor*
- *Dehumanization*
- *Legalism*
- *Intellectualism*
- *Spirit of Oppression*
- *Economic Hardship*
- *Disenfranchisement*

- *Conspiracy*
- *Greed*
- *Abortion*
- *Spirit of Religion*
- *Spirit of Miscarriage*
  Dictatorship
- *Prostitution*
  ... and more

- *Exploitation of*
  o *Children*
  o *Child pornography*
  o *Child Prostitution*
  o *Sweat Shop Labor*

CHAPTER TWO

TRANSITION

SEASONS OF TRANSITION

"Do not give up! You are right in the middle of your transition and on your way to your blessed place."

Have you ever been to the place in your life where it seemed as if everything had backfired, slowed down or even stopped? It almost appeared as though you were hanging in the midst of nowhere. This place of seemingly being nowhere is an indication that you may be experiencing a *transition!*

In the midst of your worship to warfare you may encounter major transitions in your life. Transition is the place between here and there. Transition is the space between where you were and where God is now taking you. It is the place of uncertainty, perplexity and may be occasionally coupled with fear.

It is unfortunate that in the middle of transition, many people faint, give up, turn back, or die, not realizing that this place of transition was only temporary.

Some of the conflicts and issues individuals confront when moving from worship to warfare are strongholds of the mind, called mind battles. These mind battles may manifest in the form of mental fatigue, nervous disorders, depression, fear, doubt and uncertainties. You must move swiftly to deal with these and other negative thoughts that seek to attack your mind (*See more in the Chapter 16 on Strongholds*)

While in transition, many people may encounter spiritual, financial and sexual perversion. Some fall prey to various addictions such as drugs, alcohol and sex. They may experience financial setbacks such as bankruptcy, marital distress and other dilemmas. Some people may even become numb, withdrawn or introverted, not realizing that their period of transition was only temporary.

MOVING TO THE OTHER SIDE

Jesus told His disciples to go to the other side. As soon as their journey began, the winds raged and the waves billowed. The disciples began to panic, experience doubt and were immediately ready to turn back even though Jesus had already given them their destiny, which was, the other side.

Many of you become distressed, distracted and discouraged in the midst of crossing over to your blessed place. Jesus never told them *what* was on the *other side,* or *what* they would go through while going to the other side. He just told them to go. There are blessings in obedience. God wants to take you to your blessed place.

In *Luke 10:30-37*, the parable is told of a man traveling from Jerusalem to Jericho. Jerusalem represented the house of worship and prayer. Jericho was to be his place of blessing and prosperity, however, he fell among thieves who stripped and wounded him. Many of you may be in the same position. You've been to church conferences, helped the poor, and have made invaluable sacrifices and now find yourself beaten, battered and torn.

SPIRITUAL RE-ALIGNMENT

Transition may call for major adjustments and realignments in your life, just as your car, every now and then, may experience wobbling or pulling in the wrong direction as a result of your wheels being out of line.

Sometimes, as you go through major distresses and stresses in your life, these "Hard Balls" can throw you entirely out of spiritual alignment. During these moments, if you do not realign yourself, that is, your will, you may end up straying away from God's divine will for your life.

Transition is an unforgettable place filled with complexities and uncertainties. During transition, many people lose sight of their dreams. It is during transition when nobody seems to hear you, understand you or, worst of all, agree with what you are saying and doing.

It is, therefore, vitally important that you stay your course, remembering what God had initially spoken to you and do not give up.

When in transition:
- remember the first word God spoke to you
- adjust and redirect your life
- stay your course and remain focused

- surround yourself with people who are spiritually sensitive and discerning
- Don't give up – fight to the finish!

PUSH BABY, PUSH!

You are so pregnant with destiny. What you are now experiencing are birth pangs and pains. Your water bag has broken and it is now the time to bring forth your *"promised"* child.

Your trip to the delivery room seems as though it took forever. The desire to give up overwhelms your mind, will, and emotions. Giving birth can be a treacherous experience, as both your life and the life of your unborn child are at stake. The slightest diversion can easily snatch it all away.

As you get closer to the birthing, the contractions become more and more intense. However intense the pain, it is extremely necessary in order to bring the baby forth.

It is important to note that you cannot push until you have fully dilated to at least ten (10) centimeters. Many people try to give birth to visions without going through the process. Moving at the wrong time can cause a lifetime of pain, shame, and heartache; producing life-threatening results.

The midwife always knows the right moment when you should push. Even so, you should trust the Holy Spirit to know when it is your moment.

TIMING IS EVERYTHING

It may seem easy or rather, quite normal to give birth to a baby at age fourteen (14) years. However, it may be wiser to wait until you are probably twenty-four (24) years old and married. Although age does not define wisdom, wisdom is sometimes defined with age.

I have learned over the years that waiting on God to birth a vision is important. Giving birth prematurely can sometimes cause serious birth defects and unnecessary complications.

Finally, after approximately forty (40) weeks of stretching, expanding, swelling, anticipating and waiting, you finally hear *"Push baby, push!"* With much travail you finally give birth to a wonderful baby and immediately forget the pain, pressure, and torture of the past.

Forty (40) is the period of testing, temptation and trial. Jesus went through forty (40) days of prayer and fasting and was immediately confronted by the enemy. The children of Israel took forty (40) years in the wilderness before coming into the "Promised Land."

This is your time now. You cannot waste another moment. You cannot afford to have a miscarriage neither an abortion. The vision you are pregnant with will bring so much joy to your life and the life of those around you. Position yourself; it is your time to "Push Baby, Push!" Your time of blessing is just beyond this storm. You just need to make it to the other side.

> *"For the vision is yet for an appointed time,*
> *but at the end it shall speak, and not lie:*
> *though it tarry, wait for it; because it will*
> *surely come, it will not tarry."* *(Habakkuk 2:3)*

THE POWER OF A RIGHTEOUS SEED
You must have the Faith to receive.
The Strength to conceive
And the Power to GIVE BIRTH.

CHAPTER THREE

❧

MY PERSONAL TESTIMONY:
FROM PROMISE TO POSSESSION

THE PROCESS

*"Thou has caused men to ride over our heads;
we went through fire and through water; but
thou broughtest us out into a wealthy place."*
(Psalm 66:12)

Almost every great man or woman of God will agree
that from the point God gave them a promise to the point
where it manifested or they possessed it, the process was
arduous.

The process is the place between "here and there".
It is your place of divine preparation. It is divine because God
ordained and designed it with you in mind. God has
specifically designed and tailor-made each person's process
to fit himself. God also sets in place His own procedures to
get His desired results.

No two Apostles, Prophets, Evangelists, Pastors or Teachers are alike; better yet, no two people are the same, neither are their processes "equally identical".

You must begin to embrace the fact that where you are is exactly where God wants you to be; if only for that season. Moreover, the things that you are going through were designed to prepare you for your blessed place.

You may come to a place in your process where your transition can be extremely treacherous. For the most part it is filled with tests, trials, "ups and downs". Normally, no one seems to understand you, and worst of all you do not seem to understand yourself.

SURVIVING THE TEST

I can vividly remember a time in my life when it seemed as if I was going through the worst process anybody could ever experience. I was accustomed to having lots of money, traveling on weekends, owning my own beautiful home and driving some of the best luxury cars from the Mercedes Benz, and Jaguars to BMWs.

I got married at a young age and loved my husband with every fiber of my being. We were both doing extremely well and our children were excelling in private school. My husband had his own business making thousands of dollars weekly. I, on the other hand, was an accomplished Banker and felt as if I was on top of the world.

Suddenly, my world began to fall apart. It all seemed to happen so fast, that to this day I cannot figure it all out. It was as if someone had removed the entire ground from beneath me. We went from having thousands of dollars to, within seven days, being totally bankrupt. We lost our home along with all of our apartments. The creditors collected my car and I watched painfully as they carried our furniture away piece by piece.

The following year I was diagnosed with a debilitating disorder and my doctors at the time were not sure how to cure it. After seeing several specialists, I was placed on steroids and pain-killers which had a crucial effect on my health.

I had great difficulties functioning as a wife and mother and lived in constant pain. As time passed, although I had undergone several surgical procedures, I realized that *the process was not over.* At that time, my husband and I had been married a few years. However, the thing I loved the most and cherished greatly was about to be tested.

Even though I loved God, my husband to me was everything. My marriage began spiraling out of control to the point where the pressure became so severe that during that period, I packed my bags and left. My husband's short-lived moment of unfaithfulness along with my medical health issues were so devastating that I had a nervous breakdown and was admitted to the hospital. This was one of the most horrifying times in my entire life.

While confined in the hospital and tied to my bed under 24-hour surveillance, I can remember visitations from demon spirits. They would all take turns tormenting me. These unclean spirits ranged from hurt, pain, shame, fear, self-pity, inadequacy, and worst of all; spirits of suicide and death.

I felt awful and became grossly depressed. The time I needed God most, was the time He seemed to be silent. There were no answers for what or why I was going through.

I came to realize that the Holy Spirit was teaching me a lesson which was this:

During the exam, the teacher is normally silent. In fact, she just sits there and gives you the test and waits for you to finish. She has taught the lessons and principles now you must remember how to apply them.

PAYING THE PRICE

I became a Christian at the age of twelve, started preaching at the age of sixteen and started working at the age of eighteen. I got married at the age of nineteen, had two children by the age of twenty one, had built a home and, along with my husband, was operating a multi-million dollar business by the age of twenty five.

When tragedy struck, I became frustrated because I gave my tithes and offerings liberally and had helped the poor and needy but could not find anyone to rescue me in my time of need.

Watching it all seemingly vanish right before my eyes in almost one day was heart-wrenching. I can still remember days when my husband would come home from work looking for me. I would be hiding in the closet. There would be days that I would go without eating as the constant clutches of suicide and death lurked around me.

Over the years while growing up, I had received many prophecies as to how God was going to use and bless me, but what I did not know was that I had to go through the process before the possession.

My doctor at the time, along with my husband, worked tirelessly to revive me, but it was all to no avail. It was not until one day that I was lying on my bed unable to pray or read my Bible that I began to worship God. My room became saturated with the presence of God. The Holy Spirit reminded me that He had called me to preach His word and prophesy to nations.

"SALVATION IS FREE
BUT THERE IS A PRICE TO PAY FOR THE ANOINTING."

Not only was I an "Island Girl" and the daughter of an alcoholic father, but no one in my entire family was a prophet much less had ever traveled to preach anywhere outside of my country.

Nevertheless, as I began embracing my calling, I started rebuking the unclean spirits and the thoughts, which had by this time escalated to fear, doubt, intimidation, inferiority, and low self- esteem. This team of cohorts had banned together as a demonic alliance in order to keep me in constant bondage and under intense oppression.

I began taking authority over them; loosing them from their diabolical assignments from over my life. I began decreeing and declaring my kingdom citizenship and started doing what God had called me to do.

During this time, I was not aware that the process I went through then was God preparing me for who I am now. In the midst of my process I had somehow forgotten *Psalm 66:12:*

> *"Thou has caused men to ride over our heads;*
> *we went through fire and through water: but*
> *thou broughtest us out into a wealthy place."*

AN AUTHENTIC ANOINTING

God is divine and all-powerful by Himself. In fact, when He had no one else to swear by, *He swore by Himself.* Thus, He wants to produce **authentic servants** that have had their own experiences and now walk in their own unique God-given kingdom purpose and assignment. Your kingdom purpose is the original intent or, rather, the reason for your existence.

Too many churches and believers waste time trying to imitate someone else's anointing. As a result everybody does the same thing and achieves the same results.

> *"For the earnest expectation of the creature*
> *waiteth for the manifestation of the sons of*
> *God." (Romans 8:19)*

The earth is waiting for the glorious manifestation of the sons of God. The world is looking for something different and searching for something powerful. The entire universe is anticipating the glory of God being revealed through you, me, and us - the entire Body of Christ.

THE PLIGHT OF THE BUTTERFLY

I can vividly remember a story told to me by my father many years ago as a little girl, while catching beautiful butterflies. He taught me how every stage in the butterfly's life was very important. The eggs, larvae, and pupa, though seemingly insignificant, are all necessary and vitally important to the overall growth and development of the mature, adult butterfly.

At first glance, each stage of development does not reflect the final beauty of the adult butterfly. However, the closer it reaches towards maturity, the more its beauty and grace takes shape. Removing the butterfly from its cocoon, prematurely, could disable or lead to its untimely death.

You must see yourself as this butterfly. Though you are fearfully, wonderfully and beautifully made by the Father's natural design, you have found yourself having to go through some of the ugliest stages in your early life in order for you to begin to display the beauty that lies within you.

The butterfly's ability to push itself out of the enclosed cocoon is what strengthens its wings and helps it to fly with awe, splendor and grace. However, interfering with its natural process of development by supposedly helping could cause the eventual demise of this beautiful creature.

As you continue to encounter difficulties and hardship in your life, you must remember, your test is not designed to kill you. Sometimes, you may feel as though you are the only one going through and that nobody else is there.

During this time you must remember the butterfly and allow your wings to be strengthened as you push through your own cocoons in life.

PAIN PRECEDES PLEASURE; GO THROUGH IT!
NOTHING, NOT EVEN THE PAIN, CAN BE COMPARE TO
THE GLORY, WHICH SHALL BE REVEALED IN AND
THROUGH YOU!

CHAPTER FOUR

LETTING GO OF THE PAST

THE THRESHING FLOOR

There are many postures of worship to warfare. Lying in the presence of God on the threshing floor is by far one of the most dynamic of these experiences. The threshing floor is a place, which symbolizes process and preparation. Just as the wheat was laid out and crushed on the floor to remove the husk and chaff, we too must lay before God in humility in order to be fully processed.

David used the threshing floor on many occasions to worship and seek the face of God. He understood, even as a king and warrior, the importance of coming before Him in humble adoration and sacrifice.

Our experiences in life will either help to create in us a heart of gratitude or a heart of regret. Most people spend their entire life reliving the pain and problems of their horrible past. Their unwillingness to fully release the hurt, pain and guilt, restricts and hinders them from ever being able to let go and truly worship. *(See more in Chapter 6 on The True Worshippers)*

When we allow past devastations and circumstances to linger around, even in our subconscious minds, they breed fear and insecurity, and may retard our growth socially, spiritually and even, psychologically. The painful horrors of the past may act as a noose tightly gripped and positioned around the neck. Paul admonishes us in *Galatians 5:1, "…and be not entangled again with the yoke of bondage."*

Fearful, insecure people have great difficulties in trusting others. Thus, for the most part, these people do not fully trust God. They have become so accustomed to being hurt and rejected, that they now find great difficulty in embracing or accepting the love of Jesus. Eventually, they may accept Him as Lord in their hearts, but may later reject Him as *"Kinsman Redeemer"*.

A particular young lady attended my service a few years ago. She had been used and abused her entire life. Her father abused her from the age of four years old. She later married and her husband physically and emotionally mistreated her. After these episodes of painful and distasteful encounters, she decided never to trust a man again.

Several years after the death of her husband, she met a wonderful young man. He was so captivated by her charm that he was prepared to do whatever it took to see her smile again. Because of her lifelong hurt, pain and rejection, she had major challenges receiving love and letting go of her past disappointments.

Ruth, in the book of Ruth was willing to let go of her past hurt, pains, disappointments and the death of her husband in order to worship and serve the God of Naomi. Her sister-in-law, Orpah was so devastated by her husband's death that she returned to Moab and idol worship and was never heard of again.

The day when Ruth met Boaz for the first time was not one where she was in the mall shopping, but she was in his fields gleaning amongst the reapers. Even though she was not on staff, she seized an opportunity to serve in a field that one day, unknown to her, would become her very own. When you serve *willingly*, without hidden agendas, blessings will fall on you.

GLEANING AMONGST THE REAPERS

To **glean** is to gradually collect or gather from various sources. Ruth's gleaning amongst the reapers; collecting fragments of wheat all the way out in the fields, brought her to the feet of Boaz. Her instructions from Naomi were to lay at his feet until morning. When Boaz awakened and found her at his feet, he realized that he had to quickly marry her. They got married and Boaz gave her everything she ever dreamt of. Ruth called him her **"kinsman redeemer"**.

Five Things Ruth Was Willing To Do

Firstly, she was willing to **let go** of the past. She received transformation of the mind. Secondly, she was willing to **submit herself** which means to submerge, go under and totally surrender one's will to God. Thirdly, Ruth was willing to **follow** the directions of the Holy Spirit.

She was willing to follow Naomi wherever she led her. Fourthly, she was willing to **serve** – by gleaning in the fields of His presence, gathering from here and there; praying, fasting and studying God's word. Fifthly, Ruth was willing to **lay at his feet** in worship, prayer, and warfare.

When we begin to do these things in our daily lives, then we will embrace the blessings of God. Jesus is our kinsman redeemer and when we are prepared to lay at His feet until *day break* or until our *"breakthrough day"*, we will be blessed beyond measure.

Just like David, it is necessary that we all find our threshing floor. Upon leaving, you will find an unusual state of peace and rest. To rest and to wait is to totally rely and depend on God. In addition, it is a spiritual position where your soul is in total harmony with the perfect will of God for your life. David used this method often, as he would rest in the Lord and wait patiently on Him. *(Psalm 27)*

Humility plays an integral part during worship to warfare. In the book of *Matthew 5:5*, it states that, *"Blessed are the meek: for they shall inherit the earth."* While **1 Peter 5:5** says, *"...God resisteth the proud, and giveth grace to the humble."* Further, *James 4:6* says, *"But He giveth more grace. Wherefore He saith, God resisteth the proud, but giveth grace unto the humble."* and *James 4:10* declares, *"Humble yourself in the sight of the Lord, and he shall lift you up."*

I enjoy pacing, walking up and down, while I am in warfare prayer. *(See Chapter 13 on "Marching Soldiers")* However, there is intimate worship where one lies prostrate before God, which can never be replaced.

Ruth *walked up and down* Boaz's field, claiming her territory, pulling down strongholds. She *kneeled* to pick up

the grains of wheat that fell from the reapers. She *laid out* to receive the inheritance. She *stood* to fight for and receive what God had promised her. This is what I call "spiritual militancy." After having done all to stand, Ruth stood firm on the promises of God.

FORGIVE AND FORGET

Forgive and forget are two words that always sound good together. Despite how good they sound, the question that is usually asked is it truly possible? In fact, most people may forgive, but find it extremely difficult to truly forget.

For some, the painful traumas of their childhood or relationships on the whole, almost make it seem impossible to release and "let go". In fact, society and the church have done such a "good" job in teaching you how to cover up your past, that people find it difficult to sincerely forgive and forget.

Unforgiveness or resentment can hinder you from giving or receiving love, wisdom, counsel, or a blessing from or to the person whom you have not forgiven. Therefore, forgiveness must be the first step towards a healthy recovery.

To forgive is to stop feeling angry or resentful towards somebody for a particular mistake or wrongdoing. It goes beyond just accepting or saying, "I forgive you," or "Sorry." It is totally releasing anger and resentment for whatever was done to you. It is to pardon, exonerate or "let go of."

Not forgiving, not only opens the door for the spirit of anger and resentment, but it is a clear opening for the spirit of bitterness to enter. Bitterness comes in as a result of prolonged unforgiveness. It literally takes root in the depths of your soul. Most people struggling with this spirit normally have stomach problems such as: indigestion, ulcers, heartburn, female disorders, forms of cancer, migraine headaches, and more commonly, arthritis pain, because they hold onto the hurt or pain for too long.

I can remember praying for a lady who attended our church. Week after week she would join the prayer line for some ailment or the other. On one occasion she suffered from migraine headaches, at other times she suffered from stomach ulcers and chronic arthritis pains in her joints. I was about to lay hands on her and the Holy Spirit told me not to touch her because she was not only physically sick as the doctors thought but the spirits of unforgiveness and bitterness were manifesting through these ailments.

As I called out these spirits, she fell to the ground and began to scream. I told her to call the name of the person who hurt her and let them go, in Jesus' name. For a moment she began to convulse and shake feverishly, foaming at the mouth but as soon as she was able to say the words and command the spirits of unforgiveness, anger, resentment, pain and bitterness to go, she was totally set free and never had to receive prayer for those ailments again.

BEWARE OF THE CORDS WHICH BIND

Women, for the most part, have great difficulties in totally releasing and letting go of their past, in particular, past hurts and disappointments. Because of our womb and the ability to incubate and carry a baby, it seems as though we also nurture situations, experiences, and circumstances.

Most men that I have counseled often ask the questions, "Why doesn't my wife forget what I did ten years ago?" or "Why is she still accusing me of having an affair?" My response to them was that because women are "carriers", they carry and hold tightly to every episode in their lives. One of the easiest ways to help someone forget some horrible experience may be to shower him or her with something endearing that is good or that they love.

Women, today, want more than just a kiss, some chocolates, and a good "make up" night. What they truly want is a man who knows how to worship God and lead them right into His presence. Begin celebrating and cherishing each moment you have together, worshipping, praying, sending flowers, writing love notes, and I guarantee you that your spouse will become so captivated by your love that she will forget everything else in her past.

CHAPTER FIVE

THE ULTIMATE SACRIFICE

SACRIFICE

Sacrifice is the giving up of something that is costly or of great value unto God or some other deity. In Greek, one of the words for sacrifice is *thysia (pronounced thu-se-a)* which represents the offering of spiritual sacrifices unto God. Some examples are, a sacrifice of praise *(Hebrews 13:15)*, sacrifice of thanksgiving, *(Psalm 107:22)* and more. This sacrifice is with enthusiasm and should display one's willingness to do so, not grudgingly or of necessity.

In the Old Testament, sacrifice involved the slaughtering of animals during worship unto Jehovah God, called *zâbach (pronnoucned zaw-bakh* in the Hebrew*).* In the New Testament, however, the Greek word for sacrifice is *korban* and also denoted the giving of offerings in the form of monies, turtledoves, pigeons and more.

Sacrifice also refers to the giving up of oneself. In *Romans 12:1* it states that we are to *present our bodies as a living sacrifice; holy and acceptable unto God.* You can also present your spirit and heart as a sacrifice unto God as stated in Psalm 51.

David needed the mercies of God on his side after he had sinned and wanted to offer sacrifice to God on a threshing floor. *(2 Samuel 24: 10-25)* But he refused to accept Araunah's threshing floor without it costing him something. He paid Araunah for the threshing floor and was able to use it as an altar of sacrifice unto God where He heard David's prayer and judged him with mercy.

As you see God as a Merciful Judge and the Omnipotent, Almighty, Ruler of the Universe, you will be willing to offer up to Him your very best and costly gifts, talents, time and treasures.

As believers, we worship the Lord God, Jehovah. He is our King of kings and Lord of lords. God desires sacrifice every single day. In the Old Testament, the people willingly brought daily sacrifices to the Tabernacle. In fact, they began bringing so many gifts that Moses begged them to stop for a season.

God is no longer looking for sheep, goats or heifers, but He is looking for your entire life as a sacrifice. Abraham was willing to offer Isaac on the altar of sacrifice. However, God had a ram in the bush to be used instead and blessed Abraham abundantly just for his willingness to sacrifice.

MARTYRDOM: THE ULTIMATE SACRIFICE

Jesus became the ultimate sacrifice and gave His life so that we can live. He is now requiring us in return to give our lives back to Him. God wants all of you and not just a part of you. He wants you to present your body unto Him as a living sacrifice, holy and acceptable unto God, which is your reasonable service or the least that you can do.

Sacrifice unto God will bring blessings upon your life and remove curses. You must decide right now, that every day of your life, you will find the time to offer up to God sacrificial offerings that He will be pleased with. One such sacrifice is fasting. In *Revelation 12:11*, in the lives of some believers, their sacrifices cost them their lives:

> *"And they overcame him by the blood of the Lamb, and by the word of their testimony; and they loved not their lives unto the death."*

Martyrdom is the killing of a person or people for their religious or other beliefs. A martyr in the New Testament or Greek context meant a faithful witness. This faithful witness held onto the truth he believed, willing to give his life for it as a testimony.

Jesus was very clear on the requirements needed to follow and serve Him. Serving him meant persecution and, worst of all, death. This death entailed, firstly dying to the desires of your own flesh and to the things of this world.

> *"...Except ye eat the flesh of the Son of man, and drink His blood, ye have no life in you."*
> *(John 6:53)*

There are many accounts throughout scriptures of people who may be considered as martyrs. Many of the apostles and prophets endured relentless persecution and almost all died of painful deaths. Paul, for example, was beaten on numerous occasions, stoned, shipwrecked and eventually, executed in Rome. John the Divine was dipped in hot oil and exiled to the isle of Patmos to die. John the Baptist was beheaded and Peter was crucified upside down.

In *Acts 7:54-60*, Stephen was stoned before a mocking, religious crowd and in *Revelation 2:13-21*, Jesus referred to Antipas as His faithful martyr.

In *Hebrews 11:33-38a*, it speaks candidly about many people who, by faith, died waiting for the manifestation of the promises of God:

> *[33]" (great men and women of God) who by faith subdued kingdoms, wrought righteousness, obtained promises, stopped the mouths of lions,*
>
> *[34]Quenched the violence of fire, escaped the edge of the sword, out of weakness were made strong, waxed valiant in fight, turned to flight the armies of the aliens.*
>
> *[35]Women received their dead raised to life again: and others were tortured, not accepting deliverance; that they might obtain a better resurrection:*
>
> *[36]And others had trials of cruel mockings and scourgings, yea, moreover of bonds and imprisonment:*
>
> *[37]They were stoned, they were sawn asunder, were tempted, were slain with the sword: they wandered about in sheepskins and goatskins being destitute, afflicted, tormented;*
>
> *[38]Of whom the world was not worthy;..."*

It is truly amazing to me how so many of the men and women of God of old endured great afflictions for the sake of the kingdom. On the other hand, now, in our modernized, humanistic societies, the very thought of being persecuted is unheard of and utterly disdained.

In fact, many people accept Christianity, willing to receive its blessing benefits, but would rather have nothing to do with its pain and suffering.

> [11] *"Blessed are ye, when men shall revile you and persecute you, and shall say all manner of evil against you falsely, for my sake.*
>
> [12] *Rejoice, and be exceeding glad: for great is your reward in heaven: for so persecuted they the prophets which were before you."*

Jesus reveals, in *Matthew 5:11–12* that believers would have to endure seasons of persecution but that they would also receive an eternal reward. It is unfortunate, however, that most people spend their entire lives seeking rewards here on earth. Nevertheless, most of the blame for this blunder is to be placed on leaders who refuse to preach the whole truth of the Bible.

Persecution seems to be an esteemed honor in many eastern religions and cults. In fact, most of these religions encourage their followers to be willing to give their lives as witness to their cause. It is our time, as children of the Most High, to take bold and righteous stands that by any means necessary will unashamedly preach this gospel of the kingdom.

> *"...Woe is unto me if I preach not this gospel..."*
> *(1 Corinthians 9:16)*

THE SACRIFICIAL FAST

Presenting your body unto God as a living sacrifice is what He wants more than anything. Fasting is a spiritual weapon that breaks yokes, moves the hand of God on your behalf and draws you closer to His divine will.

Fasting is the denial of or abstaining from food for biblical reasons so that the voice of God can be heard more clearly in your situations. This practice is also often employed to demonstrate the sincerity of our prayers.

"Is not this the fast that I have chosen? to
loose the bands of wickedness, to undo the
heavy burdens, and to let the oppressed go free,
and that ye break every yoke?" (Isaiah 58:6)

When you are willing to turn down your plate and humbly offer yourself as a sacrificial offering, God will receive your fast and you will experience a spiritual breakthrough at some level.

Depending on the type of results that you want, you may be compelled to fast for three, seven or twenty-one days. When you take control of your physical appetite, you take control of your spiritual appetite.

Esther fasted for three days and as a result she received clear directions from God and was able to save her people from imminent destruction.

In *Daniel 10:3*, the Scriptures reveal that Daniel's fast lasted for twenty-one days. *"I ate no pleasant bread, neither came flesh nor wine in my mouth, neither did I anoint myself at all, till three whole weeks were fulfilled."* This type of fast should be engaged whenever you are warring against territorial demons, sicknesses and disease.

44

Lastly, the forty-day fast, commonly known as the Elijah fast is sustained by bread and water. This fast is advised only under the leading of the Holy Spirit and normally undertaken at the turn of some major transition in an individual's life, for example, a call to leadership or some other divine assignment. Jesus fasted for forty days and forty nights at the inception of His earthly ministry.

Fasting is a weapon that can move the hand of God on your behalf, break yokes and draw you closer to His divine will. Much time spent in both prayer and fasting will move you through the corridors, from worship to warfare and beyond.

CHOSEN IN THE FIRE
"... many are called but few are chosen." (Matthew 22:14)

If you have never experienced the fire of God in your life, you cannot defeat principalities, Machiavellian or regional demons. A *Machiavelli spirit* is a ruling spirit that sometimes influences governments or political systems. It is very manipulative and vindictive by nature and seeks to betray the innocent, subverting entire nations. Fire is definitely a part of your progression from worship to warfare. Fire has several notable properties and characteristics.

Unlike water which soaks and wets, wind which blows and causes things to shake, rock which crushes and breaks, fire burns, consumes, sanctifies, purifies, purges, cleanses, condenses, prepares, and most significantly, it refines. God declared in *Jeremiah 23:29*, *"Is not my word like as a fire? saith the Lord; and like a hammer that breaketh the rock in pieces?"*

45

In *1 Peter 4:12* we are reminded to *"...think it strange concerning the fiery trial which is to try you, as though some strange thing happened unto you."*

I would like to submit to you that if you are going through anything that seems to be **"burning you up"** - hold on! You are in your transition, for the glory of God is about to be revealed mightily in your life.

THE FOURTH DIMENSION

I believe that there are so many dimensions attainable in the life of a believer. However, many of them could only be reached based on our lifestyles and our experiences. The morning Shadrach, Meshach and Abednego got up to worship and pray, they never dreamt they would be facing one of the biggest battles of their lives.

The instructions from the king were to *bow or burn.* They had already seen the consequences suffered by their forefathers who, by bowing down to idols had forgotten the Almighty God and whom eventually died in the wilderness. Shadrach, Meshach and Abednego were adamant and resolute in their faith, unwilling to bow to the image and was, thus, thrown into the fiery furnace.

"WHATEVER FIRE DOES NOT CONSUME, IT PURIFIES, REFINES OR PREPARES."

Shadrach, Meshach and Abednego were being prepared to experience the fourth dimension of God's glory, which only comes by fire. The furnace was heated seven times hotter but became the right climate for the presence of God to show up. God told the Church of Laodicea in the book of *Revelation 3:15* that the only way He could use them was if they were hot or cold.

However, because they were neither hot nor cold but lukewarm, He spewed them out of His mouth.   This overwhelming display of God's fiery presence changed the laws of that day from the worshipping of idols to worshipping the God of Shadrach, Meshach and Abednego

They received their promotion as a result of their kingdom militancy. You can receive yours also. *The fire of God will prepare and propel you* into your divine destiny.

CHAPTER SIX

~∞◯◯∞~

THE WORSHIPPER'S TABERNACLE

THE TABERNACLE OF DAVID

If you are going to be victorious in every area of your life, you must posture yourself as a worshipper before the Lord. As a believer, it is necessary for you to understand the importance of worship. Studying the tabernacle of David may help to bring further enlightenment. To "tabernacle" means to build a holy habitation or atmosphere where God can commune with you and you with Him. The tabernacle is a place of holy habitation, consecrated for Jehovah God to dwell in.

> *"... in him we live and move and have our being;..." (Acts 17:28)*

It is not a physical place but rather a realm of spiritual attainment, accessible only through worship. I call it the tabernacle of David.

Although he did not build a physical temple of worship, David demonstrated a lifestyle of perpetual worship. Many moments, either after he had sinned or was in need of a military strategy, he would find himself in a place of brokenness, crying out to God. No matter where he was, David knew how to "find God." He was able to move the heart and hand of God because he was a worshipper.

As a worshipper, his days in the wilderness minding his father's sheep were spent writing psalms, hymns and spiritual songs unto the Lord. David was a man after God's own heart.

When we truly love God with all our heart, worship becomes easy. It is difficult to worship God or serve anyone when you do not love them. Worship is synonymous with serving. It is a lifestyle. Thus, everything you do, in word or deed, should be done to the honor and glory of God. You cannot truly worship unless you are willing to bow down and serve. Worship is also the rendering of service to a deity. However, as a believer, it is to give service to the Lord God Jehovah totally surrendering and submitting oneself in humility and honor.

This is exactly what David did his entire life. He surrendered and submitted himself totally to the divine will of the Lord God Jehovah. To surrender is the offering up or better yet, the giving up of oneself to someone or something that is more powerful than you. A gun pointed at your face tells you to surrender, especially if you do not have one yourself. Submission is similar to the word submarine. When you submit, you are like a submarine being lowered into deep waters.

It is very important during your time of worship, that as a child of God, your will and desires remain totally under that of our Lord and King. Jesus said while praying, not my will, but thy will be done. *(Matthew 26:39)*

God deserves full control of our everyday lives. What many people do not understand is that worship is a lifestyle. This is something that should be a part of your everyday life - morning, noon and night. Although there are set days and places where you go to worship, you should still be willing to break away from your daily schedule and chores and find time to worship. Your worship is intended to be perpetual.

Even waiting until you get to church is not sufficient. Normally an average church service is an hour and a half to two hours long. This is barely sufficient time to have a substantial, life-changing worship experience.

In fact most women take that amount of time to get dressed. Thus, when people rush in and out of the presence of God there is very little deposit, much less withdrawals made.

HERE COMES THE BRIDE

In order to worship or approach the King, every worshipper must go through stages of preparation. These stages can be likened to that of a bride preparing for a lifelong, covenant relationship with her one true love. This covenant relationship usually begins with a very beautifully detailed wedding ceremony ...

Jesus often refers to His Church as a bride adorned for her husband. Preparation for the wedding, in most cases, is usually done many months or years in advance. She carefully selects the members of her bridal party, decides the location and who will participate during the ceremony.

All of the colors and details are well thought-through as she selects the fragrance for the event - either roses, lilies, tulips or whatever she enjoys most. Her dress is made to her exact fit. She watches her diet, she protects her hair and skin for all this will be a part of her final glory; months and months of preparation narrows down to one day. She barely sleeps the night before; she ensures that the minutest details are in place.

The Grand Entrance

The air is bursting with excitement and enthusiasm as her guests await her arrival. In awe and splendor with bated breath, they sit, somewhat impatiently, as the organ plays the right hymns, solemn yet sweet. She enters the door and all eyes are upon her as she gracefully walks toward the altar. In her mind, she knows these moments are precious and are to be cherished forever. She is radiant. The moment that she has anticipated for days, weeks, months, years, all her life, is finally here. Her time of preparation and sacrifice has culminated into a single magnificent and spectacular affair. She is absolutely beautiful. Her guests await with eager anticipation for the moment when she will be unveiled and her beauty revealed.

Her Garments

Her garments are pure and white. There are no spots nor are there any wrinkles. Every little detail has been stitched to define who she is. The silk, satin, lace and diamonds all converged to transform this ordinary young lady into an extraordinary vision of beauty and grace. Her darling mate accepts her hand and covenants to love her eternally.

The Royal Exchange

There is a royal exchange of vows or promises. These promises are binding and can only be broken by death; *"... to have and to hold, for richer or poorer, in sickness and in health, so long as they both shall live."* Each person must give a token to the other.

Then there is the royal exchange of rings. The ring symbolizes a never ending love, made of gold or silver signifying that even through the fire the love will still remain. The signing of the document legalizes the bond.

"The Glory"

The marriage is not complete until it has been consummated. This is the "glory." Months and months have brought them to this place. The bride presents herself to her husband. He presents himself to her, in holy intimacy. There is complete joy. Their souls become bound to each other forever.

As marriage and its consummation is a lifetime covenant between a man and a woman, so is Christ to His church. We, as His bride must begin making all the necessary preparation to embrace all of His Excellencies so that upon His return, He may present unto Himself a glorious church not having spot or wrinkle.

THE POWER OF INTIMACY

God seeks out this same intimacy with His bride, the Church. Even though worship is not something that He desires physically, He designed it to be a spiritual experience. He loves when we come before Him prepared and ready. We know that our time spent with Him will be so glorious that nothing can compare to this moment of profound splendor.

Thus, preparation is vitally important. In the Old Testament Tabernacle, the first thing you met upon entering the gate was the altar of sacrifice. The people would remain in the courtyard while the priest went to the altar to sacrifice the sheep and goat being used that day. The slaying of the sacrificial lamb might have been painful to watch but the worshipper knew that the only way to truly gain access to the presence of the Lord, God was to have sacrifice on the altar. Throughout the entire Bible, one will note that before every battle Jehovah required Israel to bring a sacrifice.

After the altar of sacrifice there was the *Laver* or the *washing basin*. The priest would wash his hands after the sacrifice, looking into the mirrors in the basin, reminding himself that he must also be cleansed. The high priest meticulously moves through the inner court or the holy place to the **golden candlesticks**, the **table of showbread and the altar of incense**. This is done while offering prayer, praise and worship to God.

The purpose of the altar of incense was to represent the sweet smelling savor and aroma produced when we worship God. Once the overwhelming aroma of worship permeates the atmosphere, the priest himself becomes intoxicated, losing consciousness of his flesh and personal needs.

The priest knows that in his flesh he cannot enter the holy of holies for there was no doorway of entry beyond the veil. He must climax to a realm in his worship until he, even unknowing to himself, is *translated* behind the veil - right into the very presence of God.

THE HOLY OF HOLIES

In the holy of holies there is only the Ark of the Covenant, Aaron's budding rod, and two tablets of stone and manna. The sacrifice that was made in the outer court, if accepted, would cause the shekinah glory to fall. The worshipper now knows that he can leave the presence of his king, equipped for **W.A.R.F.A.R.E**: **W**arrior **A**rmed and **R**eady to **F**ight **A**nnihilating the **R**eal **E**nemy.

The holy of holies is the highest level of spiritual communion where every believer should aspire to attain. It is the very presence of God and, better yet, the essence of His glory.

Although the physical temple described in the Old Testament no longer exists, God expects each of us to elevate to a place of complete oneness with Him. It is a place where we are no longer struggling in our carnal flesh, but where we abide confidently in His presence. The cherubim that guard the mercy seat also guard our souls and position us to receive God's matchless grace and bountiful favor.

THE TRUE WORSHIPPERS
"God is a Spirit; and they that worship Him must worship Him in spirit and in truth."
(John 4:24)

" ...for the Father seeketh such to worship Him." (John 4:23b)

Jesus emphasizes here that two of His requirements for worship are that we worship Him in spirit and in truth, not in our carnal way of thinking that is based on what we think or how we feel that it should be done.

Every believer must understand that there is no cohesiveness between the spirit and the flesh; either you are spiritual or you are carnal. There is always enmity between the two – they will never agree. As light is to darkness, east is to west, summer is to winter and hot is to cold, so is the spirit to the flesh. The spirit and flesh are irreconcilable.

The woman at the well thought that Jesus was like all the other fleshly men she would normally meet at the well. She was very religious and thought that her dissertation of the geographical and genealogical history of her forefathers, the well and the mountain would have impressed Jesus.

However, it was quite the opposite. Jesus took two minutes and spoke of the living water that He represented. This same woman began gasping for a drink of that living water. He spoke to her about the five husbands she had and that the one she was now holding on to, was not even hers.

Many times people come to God claiming to be true worshippers but, they are married and mentally, emotionally, or physically soul tied to at least five systems. These five systems may include lodges, fraternities, clubs, habits, families, friends, career, denominations and the political arena.

Jesus wants us to be totally sold out to and married only to Him. A true worshipper seeks only to please the one he or she adores. When the woman at the well fully understood who Jesus was, she immediately divorced all the other "husbands" and told them to come and see the Christ. *True worshippers seek relationship, not religion.*

THE SPIRITUAL FRAGRANCE OF WORSHIP

When Mary Magdalene, a famous prostitute of her day, bought her alabaster box of ointment, she poured it upon the feet of Jesus, not knowing that some day she would reap an eternal blessing. This act of sacrificial worship would have her name mentioned everywhere the gospel is preached. The one box of fragrance she released to Jesus brought eternal blessings to her for the rest of her life. God is looking for this special fragrance everyday from His children.

Mary's washing of Jesus' feet with her tears and drying them with her hair was, in my opinion, one of the most outstanding acts of worship to warfare anyone could ever display. Her tears represented all the years of joy, hurt and pain she had stored up.

The flow of the ointment from the broken alabaster box was her willingness to release these "tears" at her Savior's feet. Drying his feet with her hair represented the release from every spirit of pride and vainglory from herself, giving it all over to God.

ONE MEASURE OF WORSHIP IS WORTH MORE THAN MOMENTARY PLEASURE. GIVE GOD WORSHIP AND HE WILL GIVE YOU A LIFETIME OF BLESSINGS BEYOND MEASURE.

It is always the fear of getting beyond the people and obstacles of obstruction that would try to hinder you from gaining entrance into the king's chamber. Once you enter, that is all that matters. Your job as a living sacrifice is now to release a sweet aroma; a fragrance never smelt before by this Almighty King. This fragrance must be potent and powerful enough to saturate the entire room, lifting Him off of His Royal throne.

At this point, you must maintain your composure and posture. ***Your composure involves*** not being cognizant of yourself but maintaining your focus on the one you seek to embrace. Thus, you should remain peacefully yielded.

Your *posture on the other hand* denotes that this holy worshipper knows that even in the humble kneeling position, the heart is more inclined to give the Sovereign King all that He deserves. It is the state of total surrender and pure submission of one's will and desires to that of the King, which brings His favor upon your life.

Posture in worship is therefore more the position of one's soul (mindset and will) than it is of body. Even though the kneeling, yielded servant humbly bows, the surrender of the heart and its fragrance in sincere worship produces more than can ever be desired from His Eminence, the King.

YOUR TIME OF WORSHIP

There is absolutely a time and a season for every thing under the sun. "A time to laugh and a time to weep, a time to embrace and a time to refrain from embracing, a time of peace and a time of war." *(Ecclesiastes 3)*

"He teacheth my hands to war, so that a bow of steel is broken by mine arms." (Psalms 18:34)

As a believer you must know when to worship and when to warfare. Everyone that God called came to Him as a worshipper but later became a warrior. Worship is considered the pre-requisite for gaining entry and obtaining favor in the King's presence.

This notable act of coming through the garden and into the courtyard, getting clearance from the gatekeepers, passing the door and bellman, pushes you right into the view of His Majesty. Now that you are in His presence, you are free to worship.

58

The Royal Scepter & Chamber

In the royal chamber the king expects oneness. It is personal yet enchanting. His expectation is that of authenticity, simply meaning, "be yourself, my child and seek not to give me what you have given to others." He wants fresh *"scent-say-tions."* He never compares yours to that of anyone else. Your gift to Him is unique and cherished. Your sacrifice of spirit, soul and body is received once you see the royal scepter extended towards you.

The stretching forth of the royal scepter is now the new strength, and the power anointing that you receive. It is at this point where you would have lost yourself totally in your worship, unaware of the words coming out of your mouth and emanating out of your spirit. Your worship now becomes warfare. You are poured out and totally yielded to whatever He wants you to do.

Kings and Queens

"Presenting your gifts of worship to Him will bring greater blessings to you."

Kings and Queens always exchange gifts. Their loyalty to each other was not only measured by the weight of the gift but by the depth of love with which it was given. King Solomon and the Queen of Sheba were primary examples of this as King Solomon's gift to her caused her to faint.

She was so impressed by what she saw in his kingdom that she became overwhelmed. The Queen of Sheba may have come with an evil intention, but she left with a divine impartation.

In *Revelation 1:6, God calls us kings and priests*. In *1 Peter 2:9*, He calls us a chosen generation, a royal priesthood, an holy nation, and a peculiar people. When you come before the King of kings in worship and present your gifts of honor, God in return releases His splendor and glory back to you. When God's glory is presented back to us or His presence shows up, most people become slain or physically weak. In fact, Daniel fell as dead *(Daniel 8:17)*, so did John the Divine Revelator *(Revelation 1:17)* and Joshua when he saw the angel in chapter five of the book of Joshua *(Joshua 5:14)*.

My friend, God desires to reveal Himself to you. You must remain in a state of spiritual preparedness for when His glory shows up in your life.

WORSHIP PRODUCES SACRIFICE,
SACRIFICE ON THE ALTAR IGNITES FIRE,
FIRE BRINGS TRANSFORMABLE CHANGE AND THE
MANIFESTATION OF THE SUPERNATURAL.

MANIFESTATION OF THE SUPERNATURAL

"And call ye on the name of your gods, and I
will call on the name of the Lord: and the God
that answereth by fire, let him be God..."
(1 Kings 18:24)

The world is waiting to see the God of Elijah show up and show off His supernatural power. Elijah the prophet was human just as we all are, but he walked in such a powerful level of kingdom authority that even the atmospheric elements were subject to him.

Not only was he able to stop the rain, but, also through the power of God, he was able to call fire down from heaven defeating the false prophets of Baal and those of the Groves who ate at Jezebel's table.

This supernatural display of God's sovereign power only comes after a lifetime of preparation and processing. God, Himself shows up and demonstrates His power in the life of someone who is willing to offer sacrifices to Him. Elijah spent most of his days living in caves and seeking the face of Jehovah God. Whenever the king wanted a word from him, he would have to send a search out for Elijah.

As a true worshipper you must seek to spend quality time away in the presence of Almighty God if you are going to manifest His supernatural power in your life.

The supernatural goes beyond what you are physically or naturally able to see or do in your own strength. It is, therefore, God intervening to display His omnipotence and sovereignty. The supernatural may involve miracles, signs and wonders and may affect an individual or an entire crowd.

Many of these powerful displays of the supernatural can be seen throughout the scriptures; from healing the blind, cleansing the lepers to the feeding of thousands. All were the supernatural workings of God.

The Miracle Of The Four Lepers

In *2 Kings 7*, Israel was experiencing one of its worst famines ever. The entire city was in a state of hopelessness, to the point where people ate dove's dung and even their children, in order to survive.

Elisha, the prophet, prophesied, in spite of the famine, that by the following day, they would be able to buy flour and barley in the gates again.

Everyone knew that there was no way naturally possible for this to be done, considering their present circumstances. However, God used four lepers, who were left to die outside the city, to enter the Syrians camp to initiate a supernatural experience.

God supernaturally allowed the footsteps of the lepers to sound, to the Syrians, as a mighty army approaching with chariots and horses, thus forcing them to abandon their tents full of food, clothing, gold and silver. The lepers were totally amazed at the supernatural discovery and ate until they were full. They sent a message to the King about their supernatural blessing and the entire city benefited. Jehovah God had done what no man could do.

He is the God of the supernatural and, contrary to some erroneous beliefs; God is still working miracles today. He wants to do the same in your life, especially in the areas of your life in which you feel helpless, hopeless or weak. As you worship and earnestly seek the face of the Almighty God, He will perform wonders in your life; in your finances and in your family, only trust Him today as you offer Him the ultimate sacrifice.

CHAPTER SEVEN

DIMENSIONS FROM WORSHIP TO WARFARE

POSITIONS OF WORSHIP

As a believer, as long as you are in this world, there is going to be some level of spiritual warfare in your life. But as you worship, your personal time that was spent in worship prepares you for victory during your time of battle and spiritual warfare. There are a number of different positions one can assume in worship. Most worshippers start out kneeling, others lay prostrate before Him and then there are those who cannot help but to break out in a dance.

This worshipping prince or princess who has broken out into a dance knows that he or she has the king's full attention. The worshipping, dancing prince or princess can now move into a realm of freely expressing his or her inner thoughts by sporadic movements before the King.

The release of fresh anointing oil compels and propels the worshipper, equipping him for a higher dimension of warfare. He or she is no longer frail and fragile, but their strength is now renewed as they soar on eagles' wings to greater dimensions of worship. The worshipper now takes on the innate nature of the King and is empowered by His glory to become more than a conqueror.

"Even the youth shall faint and be weary and the young man shall utterly fall: But they that wait upon the Lord shall renew their strength; they shall mount up with wings as eagles; they shall run, and not be weary; and they shall walk, and not faint." (Isaiah 40:30-31)

THE GREATER THE INTENSITY OF THE WORSHIP, THE GREATER THE FRAGRANCE THAT POURS OUT!

In Hebrews 4:16, the Spirit of God admonishes us to *"come boldly unto the throne of grace"*. However, it was your *petition* or intercession request to come before the king, which extends the grace of God to give you intimate access to His presence. Just as Esther took twelve months before she came before the king, you must also likewise prepare. Your seasons of *preparation* **will** dress you for His presence

Remember that you are now a warrior. It is important that each warrior remembers what it took to get into the presence of God and commit to developing a lifestyle of worship as you perpetually prepare for His presence.

IT IS EASIER TO 'PREPARE' THAN TO HAVE TO "REPAIR!"

Do not forget it was also the *process* that prepared you to have intimacy with God. Without pride and false submission, you entered in, bypassing the opinions of other people, your own personal issues and gained you *Access.*

Your brokenness of spirit and renewed mind are all credentials that elevated you to dimensions of royalty.

Your presentation of gifts and accolades were well received and are never to be forgotten. You must therefore maintain a lifestyle of perpetual worship if you are going to continue to experience the presence and power of God.

A GREATER DIMENSION OF WORSHIP

A dimension is literally a spiritual world that exists with realms, spheres and levels. It is a place of coming into by way of higher thoughts. These higher thoughts may be unfolded or unveiled in time through understanding dreams, ideas, visions and the Word of God. Dimensions unfold by the revelation of the Spirit of God. When you get a greater revelation or understanding of God or His Word, you enter into a higher dimension.

You also experience a greater dimension of the Spirit of God as you seek Him as you endure your difficulties and hardships. Every time you go through something in life, it is supposed to take you closer to God. For this reason, as you are going through your tests and trials, you are admonished to draw closer to God; remembering that your trials are designed to press out a deeper level of worship in your life.

Thus, the twenty dimensions From Worship To Warfare can only be realized or achieved based on your time spent in the presence of God. Although there are several levels of praise, I believe that there are over twenty dimensions "from worship to warfare". You must ask the Holy Ghost to help you to achieve them.

Worship may sometimes be compared to entering into a house, going through corridors, defeating the plots, plans and strategies of the enemy along the way and finally entering the chambers of God. Remember, worship is a powerful expression of your spirit to God and is further accomplished through prayer. Therefore, we cannot worship without praying and we cannot effectively pray without worshipping.

There are several things you can experience as a result of availing yourself to worship God. Seeking the face of God and practicing a dedicated lifestyle of Worship can:
- release the blessings of God to flow in your life
- bring deliverance from depression and oppression
- drive away evil spirits
- usher you into the very presence of God
- release the gifts of the Spirit to operate or manifest in your life
- reveal the very essence of who God is
- bring glory to God
- enhance spiritual intimacy
- activate and release the prophetic mantle upon your life *(2 Kings 3:15)*
- set ambushments against your enemies and confusion in the midst of the battle
- bring deliverance from the enemy
- destroy the yokes of the devil and break chains, by the anointing
- increase your desire for more of God
- bring your total being (body, soul, and spirit) in perfect alignment with the will of God for your life *(1 Thessalonians 5:23)*

TWENTY (20) DIMENSIONS FROM WORSHIP TO WARFARE

Please note that these dimensions can only be achieved through focused, consistent prayer. The following twenty dimensions have been designed by God to navigate you to a place of spiritual elevation in Him:

1) BROKENNESS: You can only truly worship God when you become broken. Brokenness is a yielded submitted position of pouring out oneself in the presence of God *(Psalm 51:17)*. You see yourself as incomplete and undone before Him. This brokenness can manifest through praise.

Towdah (pronounced tow-daw) – is a Hebrew word for praise that means coming before God is total adoration; cupping and extending your hands before Him in a sacrifice of praise, glory, honor, and majesty

2) REPENTANCE: It is returning wholly to your spiritual place in God. It is also a complete change of heart, casting off every weight and the sin which so easily besets you. (Psalm 51:10)

Towdah (pronounced tow-daw) – towdah praise in this sense means confession

3) SURRENDER: To totally give oneself back to the will of God. At this level of worship your attitude would be "...not as I will, but as thou wilt." (Matthew 26:39).

(Continue to Towdah, giving Him praise, glory, honor, and majesty) At this level Towdah (praise and worship) continues.

4) BOWING: A symbol of your reverential appreciation and acknowledgement of God as Sovereign, as Supreme, as Majestic, as King of kings and Lord of lords in your life.

Shachah (pronounced shaw-khaw) - this is the Hebrew word meaning to bow down before God in reverence to His majesty. (Job 1:20)

5) KNEELING : This is dropping on your knees and upon your face in humble adoration before your King desiring to be filled even more with His Spirit.

Barak (pronounced Baw-rak) – is the Hebrew word meaning to kneel before the Lord in praise, glory, honor, and majesty

6) ROCKING: This is a back and forth movement either sitting or kneeling before God. Hannah in her desperation to have a child demonstrated this while praying in the temple. Eli the priest thought she was drunk. *(1 Samuel 1:14)* *(See more in Spiritual Intoxication)*

Continue to Barak (praise God) and give Him glory, honor, and majesty (Barak continues at this level of worship)

7) SPIRITUAL INTOXICATION: To become overwhelmed and seemingly drunk in the Spirit surrendering your will totally to God. It is at this point where you are no longer in control of your thoughts, your speech, or your emotions. When you reach this point, you are at the road of no return. You are no longer cognizant of the time and, in some cases, where you are.

The Spirit of God has guided you into the Z.O.N.E. - *Zenith Operation Now Engaged!* The Z.O.N.E. represents one of the highest points in your worship. The Z.O.N.E. is the place where you become *consumed and possessed* by His presence and His power. You are a worshipping warrior in the realm of the spirit engaged in one-on-one combat in a fight - to win.

Thillah (pronounced Teh-hil-law) - is a Hebrew word that represents a spiritually intoxicated level of praise before the Lord – during this level of praise offering you may begin to sing spiritual songs to God in your native tongue or heavenly language; giving Him praise, glory, honor, and majesty.

8) TRAVAILING/CRYING OUT : A cry which comes from the depth of your soul releasing verbal expressions, not giving up until a breakthrough is in sight. In Isaiah 66:7 the Word of God lets us know that *"When Zion travails, then she brings forth children."*

Shabach (pronounced shaw-bakh) - is a Hebrew word which means to express your worship by loud, boisterous tones; shouting unto the Lord, crying out with a voice of triumph as you continue to give Him praise, glory, honor, and majesty (Psalm 47:1)

9) OUTPOURING OF THE SOUL: It is at this time that you are praying in the spirit, groaning in a language *(a heavenly language)* unknown to self but understood by God, out of your belly. At this point, deep is calling unto deep, where you are totally broken and yielded in the presence of God.

Thillah (pronounced Teh-hil-law) – is a Hebrew word that represents a spiritually intoxicated level of praise before the Lord – during this level of praise offering you may begin to sing spiritual songs to God in your native tongue or heavenly language; giving Him praise, glory, honor, and majesty.

Continue to give Him praise, glory, honor, and majesty; you are in your Tehillah place again with Zomar (incorporating instruments)

10) RESTING: *"Rest in the Lord, and wait patiently for Him."* (Psalm 37:7). To enter into the rest of God is the place where you are no longer fighting in your own strength, but you are confident that God is working for you. It is a place of profound peace and tranquility. The Dimensions from 10 to 12 are dimensions of spiritual camouflage. It is during this stage that the enemy thinks you are defeated because you are in a rest mode. Unknown to him, you are only being refueled by the Spirit of God for the final round.

Shaqat (pronounced shaw-kat) – this is a Hebrew word which represents a resting, settled worship posture; laying before God silently, listening to the voice of God through the ears of the Spirit and continue to give Him praise, glory, honor, and majesty (Isaiah 30:15... in quietness and confidence shall be your strength;...)

11) WAITING/BEING STILL: Psalm 27:14 *"Wait on the Lord: be of good courage,..."* It is in this dimension that you are not in a hurry. You are not absolutely sure about the next move so you stand still waiting for clear directives from God as Joshua did.

Continue to Shaqat before Him as you give Him praise, glory, honor, and majesty

12) LAYING OUT: It is at this stage that you seek to dispossess, possess and receive the next level of instructions. Lying on the threshing floor is the lowest place one can go in humility before God. Laying before Him restores your soul and gives you spiritual insight into the realm of the spirit. *(See the Threshing Floor in Chapter 4)*

Shakab (Hb - Shaw-kab) - Lie down for rest; cast down and lay thyself down (Ruth 3:4-14; Exodus 16:33) As you lay and rest in His presence continue to give Him praise, glory, honor, and majesty

13) PURSUING: It is a relentless pressing deeper and going further into the presence of God. This is a moment of intensified warfare and should be done tenaciously. *(1 Samuel 30)* In your pursuit you may engage *angelic assistance*. Michael is the archangel assigned with a host of angels to fight on our behalf and hearken to our command to defeat the enemy.

"...angels, that excel in strength, that do His commandments, harkening unto the voice of His word." (Psalm 103:20)

"Who maketh His angels spirits; His ministers a flaming fire."(Psalm 104:4)

Râ-daph (pronounced raw-daf) *is a Hebrew word that means to pursue or to run after; chase in the realm of the spirit (1 Samuel 30:10; Joshua 10:19) As you Ra-daph the Lord continue to give Him praise, glory, honor, and majesty*

14) MARCHING TO AND FRO (A WORSHIPPING WARRIOR DANCE): God told Abraham, wherever the soles of his feet went was his. It is at this stage that your blessing has been released but the enemy is now trying to block, stop and hinder it from manifesting in your life. You must now become spiritually more militant and aggressive than ever before. You must be willing to march in the realm of the spirit, aggressively bombarding the enemy's camp. *(See more in Joshua 6)*

Taqua (pronounced taw – kah)– is a Hewbrew that means to dance sporadically after marching consumes one's entire being. David danced before the Lord with all his might (2 Samuel 6:14-16) Continue to give Him praise, glory, honor, and majesty

15) INFILTRATION: Portals and spheres have now been opened in the realm of the spirit. This is your access point and you must move swiftly. These portals and spheres will not remain open for long. (See the account of Jacob's portal through a dream in *Genesis 32:24-32*) Go in now and seize what is rightfully yours.

You are now engaged in spiritual, military war. This is your spiritual military war. This is your apostolic calling to regain territories.

Tsaba (pronounced Saw-baw) This is a Hebrew word which represents that you are now engaged in spiritual military war. The Greek word strateia (pronounced strat-i-ah) speaks to an attitude or posture of spiritual military service and your apostolic calling to regain territories. (1 Samuel 28:1; 1Timothy 1:18) Continue to give Him praise, glory, honor, and majesty

16) BINDING: In order to defeat the enemy you must first bind him. Matthew 18:18 says *"... Whatsoever ye shall bind on earth shall be bound in heaven; and whatsoever ye shall loose on earth shall be loosed in heaven."* Binding renders the enemy powerless, disabling his plans and tactics.

Dēsmĕuo (pronounced des-myoo-o) – this Greek word means to enchain, tie, bind ar imprison the enemy in Jesus' name as you continue to give God praise, glory, honor, and majesty

17) LOOSING/BREAKING THE CHAINS: Once you have bound the enemy, you must "fire" him, making him aware that he is loosed from his assignment. This involves breaking chains of generational curses, ungodly soulties, vows, pledges, agreements, covenants, and promises. Disarming him relinquishes the power of demonic gate-keepers and positions you to reassign heavenly warriors and watchers.

Luó (pronounced Loo-o) – this is a Greek word which represents to loosen, break up or destroy, dissolve, melt, put off as you continue to give Him praise, glory, honor, and majesty (John 11:44)

18) DECREEING AND DECLARING You must now begin to emphatically speak forth into manifestation your desires, overriding the schemes and plans of the enemy and putting into effect kingdom laws. *"Thou shalt also decree a thing, and it shall be established..."* (Job 22:28).

"For by thy words thou shalt be justified, and by thy words thou shalt be condemned." (Matthew 12:37)

"... it (my Word) shall not return unto me void, but it shall accomplish that which I please..." (Isaiah 55:11)

Exegeomai (pronounced Ex-ayg-eh-om-ahee) – This is a Greek word which means to declare or tell aloud (Acts 15:12).

Halal (pronounced haw-lal) – This is a Hebrew word which means the act of clamorously, foolishly, celebrating and declaring your imminent victory as you continue to give Him praise, glory, honor, and majesty.

19) OVERTAKING/OVERTHROWING: In the context of a military strategy this means to seize and to fight. Jacob wrestled all night until he received his breakthrough (Genesis 32). David had the same experience in 1 Samuel 30. Remember, you must remove demonic powers off of the throne in the areas you are praying for (such as marriages, families, jobs, businesses, finances, and others) and release the Spirit of God to take full control.

Nasag (pronounced Naw-sag) is a Hebrew word which means to overtake; take hold of what is rightfully yours as you continue to give Him praise, glory, honor, and majesty (Exodus 15:9; Joshua 2:5)

20) RECOVERING ALL/PREVAILING: As you attain this level of worship, you now have the confidence that you have regained all that the enemy has stolen, along with full compensation and interest of at least a seven fold increase. You know beyond the shadow of a doubt that it is now your season and time for total restoration or victory.

Açaph (pronounced Aw-saf) – This is a Hebrew word that means the regaining and gathering back of everything; that was once lost or stolen. (2 Kings 5:3-11) You will recover all as you continue to give Him praise, glory, honor, and majesty

CHAPTER EIGHT

A PLACE IN GOD

SPIRITUAL VISION

Spiritual Vision is called 20/20 Vision as your life transitions from Worship To Warfare. When you attain spiritual vision you are now a "twenty-foot giant" in the realm of the spirit. You are now able to clearly discern and, beyond the shadow of every doubt, know God's divine will for your life. When you have climaxed and have elevated to this realm from worship to warfare, you will have total peace and spiritual power.

You are now able to see in the realm of the spirit and are able to accurately discern what spirits are in operation in your life and the lives of others. Your spiritual antennas are alert and sensitive to the slightest movement in the spirit realm.

As defined in *1 Corinthians 2:14-15,* you have now progressed to a place of spiritual maturity:

> 14*"But the natural man receiveth not the things of the Spirit of God: for they are foolishness unto him: neither can he know them, because they are spiritually discerned.*
>
> 15*But he that is spiritual judgeth all things, yet he himself is judged of no man."*

and again in *Hebrews 5:13–14:*

> 13*"For every one that useth milk (elementary principles of doctrine) is unskillful in the word of righteousness: for he is a babe.*
>
> 14*But strong meat belongeth to them that are of full age, even those who by reason of use have their senses exercised to discern both good and evil."*

Your peace is as a result of being able to see, spiritually, what no one else around you sees. This spiritual discernment and foresight enable you to do what ordinarily could not be done. Seeing is different from having vision. We walk by faith and not by sight. *(2 Corinthians 5:7)*

Vision goes beyond your natural ability to see. Spiritual vision and insight enables you to fight wisely and not foolishly. It makes you become fully aware of the enemy you are fighting and shows you precisely how to defeat him. In *2 Corinthians 2:11 the Word of God warns that we are not to be ignorant of satan's devices.*

Most of the problems we see happening around us originate from the kingdom of darkness. The social ills of drugs, violence, abuse and the exploitation of children are the results of the invisible works of demonic spirits. When believers begin to intercede and bombard heaven, God will open their eyes to see the real enemy behind the problem.

Have you ever been to a point where you needed an answer to a problem or some monies to pay a bill? You may have spent the entire day calling everyone you knew but received no help. You may remember that you never got directions until you prayed. Satan's job is to bring distractions to you, so that you would not see your way through.

Worship and intercession open this portal and give us access. Elijah asked God to open his servant's eyes so that he could see that there was more with them than the enemies that had set themselves against them. Elijah's perception was solely based on his faith in God that he would protect them and defeat their enemies.

It is God's desire for us to see into the invisible realm. Demon spirits are there but there are also angels warring on our behalf to help bring to pass God's divine will in our lives.

When we know how to worship, intercede and warfare we experience sweatless victories. In 2 Chronicles 20 when the Ammonities came against King Jehosophat and the children of Israel, they were out-numbered. King Jehosophat set his face to seek the Lord and experienced one of the greatest military victories recorded in Biblical history, without raising a single sword or javelin. God had sent invisible spiritual ambushment in the midst of their enemy and they destroyed each other.

"Worship is a very important component or element of prayer. You cannot pray effectively until you have worshipped and you cannot worship until you have prayed."

Thus, worship and intercession changes the atmosphere and makes any environment conducive for miracles, revealing the glory of God.

A PLACE IN GOD
(THE CLIFT OF THE ROCK)

What the twenty-first century believer is missing is the full manifestation of the glory of God. If you would be totally honest, your desire in life is to see the shekinah glory of God show up in every area of your life.

However, it would seem as if, every time the Holy Spirit brings us to a place in God to experience this glory, satan, somehow seeks to intercept this move by throwing busyness, distractions, confusion, contention and rebellion in your way.

God longs to manifest His Glory in ways unimaginable to His children, but it comes with a price. God says to His children, "There is a place by me, *it's in the clift of the rock"* *(Exodus 33:22).* It is there between a rock and a hard place; you will find me, see me and hear my voice. It is a place beyond the people, beyond the veil of your flesh, your finances, situations and circumstances.

In some translations of the Bible, it mentions the phrase "cleft of the rock" which represents a place of protection. However, in my experience, I have found that God takes prophets and places them in the "clift of the rock" which is sometimes an uncomfortable and unfamiliar place in order to reveal a greater glory of His presence.

God is always there waiting, willing and ready to reveal Himself to His beloved. You must strive to find your secret place in God, your clift of the rock. It is place of spiritual ascension to which one attains as a result of spending quality time communing with Him. You must be prepared to break away and consecrate a specific place for this communion.

Some ideal locations may be a prayer closet, your personal office, a remote wilderness or beach or a brief sabbatical at a resort. Whenever you are able to get away, alone in His presence, this can be classified as your *"clift in the rock."*

Consecrating time and a place to meet God is the beginning of a powerful journey, one you will never forget. It was out of this place that both Moses and David received divine revelations and direction for the next chapters in their lives.

Moses asked God to show him His ways in order to know Him better and God led him to a *clift of the rock.* Many times people desire to experience the glory of God in their lives but are not prepared to pay the painful price. The price Moses paid, his clift, was laborious days of fasting, praying and spending time alone in the mountains seeking the face of God.

On the other hand, the children of Israel ate, drank and were merry and only knew the acts of God, whereby Moses knew His ways. Find the time and the place and I promise you, God will meet you there. Where there is a will there is definitely a way. God has a prepared place for a prepared people, but you have a part to play in building this place. If you build it, He will come!

BEWARE OF DISTRACTIONS

One of satan's plans is to distract the anointed from the things of God so that less time is spent seeking and serving Him. As long as Peter kept his eyes on Jesus he walked on water. When he began to look at the wind and the waves he began to sink.

Another example was Mary and Martha. Mary sat at Jesus' feet while Martha was busy doing a good thing but at the wrong time. Sitting at Jesus' feet represents the time each believer should spend in the presence of God, worshipping and gleaning from His presence. It is at His feet that you leave empowered with the ability to stand on your own two feet and accomplish His mandate in your life.

Marthas who do not spend time at Jesus' feet, find themselves distracted and frustrated by every little thing. Sometimes we can become very "busy" doing nothing, but still have no time to seek God. The Bible says, *"Mary chose the better part."* In the midst of your busy schedule, stop for a brief moment to worship and you will experience such profound glories that the "task at hand" becomes effortless.

There is a season and a time in your life when God calls you to walk with people especially family, friends, co-workers and there is another season in your life where He may call you to walk alone.

I can personally remember those days of having to walk alone, wanting to fit into the crowd, wanting to be accepted and do what everybody else was doing. There would be days when the Holy Spirit would restrain me to a time of seeking Him. These were not all joyful days. In fact I can clearly remember feeling lonely, rejected, and alienated from many of my friends, even those in ministry.

MY PERSONAL CLIFT

My clift was a painful and hard place, but it was there where I found my greatest peace and fulfillment in God.

80

These were the times that I experienced some of my most profound moments in Him.

- *My clift was*

    Being called to the ministry at a young age, wanting to be accepted but never able to fit in

- *My clift was*

    Spending many long and lonely nights fasting and broken in the presence of God while everyone else seemed to be "enjoying life"

- *My clift was*

    Being misunderstood, misrepresented, and feeling rejected

- *My clift was*

    A place of isolation and intense preparation

Some of my greatest messages were birthed out of many hours of brokenness, despair, and darkness. In the midst of all of this I believe that that was when I heard God's voice clearest. Many times it was even difficult for me to find what I call "the light switch." I had to learn to navigate through my dark seasons and trust God in every moment of my life.

I thank God for my *"clift in the rock" (my hiding place).* You should take the time to seek Him for yours. In *Exodus 33:22,* Moses found this place. In Psalms 91, David dwelt in this place – it was the secret place of the Most High God.

BEYOND MEASURE

Many people limit or restrict the flow of God in their life because they erroneously approach God with a religious mindset. Just like the Pharisees, because of their religious mindset, they tend to measure everything that they do for God. Throughout the scriptures, the Pharisees often boasted of their times of prayer, the garments they wore, how much they gave or on what they could not do on the Sabbath day. All of this was in an effort to glorify their religious laws and customs...so they measured everything.

In this same manner, some people may even become exact as it relates to the things of God. For example, some people hold fast to strict, legalistic views rather than seeking a deeper relationship with God.

God has unlimited blessings in store for you, but more than all He has an unlimited supply of the anointing that He desires to pour into you...*without measure!*

Therefore, you should not measure your time spent in worship and prayer because one day in the presence of the Lord is better than a thousand anywhere else. *(Psalm 84:10)* To measure, calculate or count your experiences in God may cause you to nullify every possibility of a tremendous overflow of the anointing in your life.

> *"A measure of wheat for a penny, and three measures of barley for a penny;...and see thou hurt (touch) not the oil and wine."*
> *(Revelation 6:6)*

> *"...Eye hath not seen, nor ear heard neither have entered into the heart of man, the things which God hath prepared for them..."*
> *(1 Corinthians 2:9)*

The blessings that God has in store for you, His child, and especially wants to pour out when you worship and warfare cannot be measured. All the trials, tests, and tribulations you have endured in your life qualify you to receive an immeasurable anointing from God.

People who have not been through anything in life have little or no appreciation or understanding of your pain. Neither will they have any appreciation when God blesses you.

You must, therefore, begin to see the value of the oil on your own life. The oil represents the intangible anointing and the wine represents the tangible wealth that will flow in your life *(Revelation 6:6).*

"... if I will not open you the windows of heaven, and pour you out a blessing, that there shall not be room enough to receive it."
(Malachi 3:10)

CHAINBREAKING PROPHETIC UTTERANCE

I believe that the time is coming and now is upon us, where it will be difficult for anyone to measure or constrain the move of God. I say this because there is going to be a release of glory that eyes have not seen neither ears heard of; just as it was on the day of Pentecost and the day after Pentecost. Wherever the devil has sought to place restrictions and limitations on the life of the believer, God is going to release an anointing to break His people beyond the enemy's demonic barriers. In this season, the Holy Spirit is coming without constraints....He is pouring Himself out without measure.

PART II

SPIRITUAL WARFARE

CHAPTER NINE

❧∞◦❀◦∞❧

SPIRITUAL WARFARE

UNDERSTANDING SPIRITUAL WARFARE

"...though we walk in the flesh, we do not war after the flesh."

For the weapons of our warfare are not carnal but mighty through God to the pulling down of strongholds." (2 Corinthians 10:3-4)

We are living in a day and time when it would seem as though many people forget that we are engaged in a constant battle. Some people believe that once they become a believer and are filled with the Holy Ghost, that it is smooth sailing for the rest of their lives.

Some people feel that the devil automatically leaves you alone, all of your bills will be supernaturally paid, your children will be obedient and husbands and wives will treat each other just as the Bible says. If that were so, then we should just all go to sleep, do not pray, fast or even study the Word of God.

Satan, through his diabolical tactics and plans has convinced many believers that God does not want them to be spiritually aggressive or radical in their faith. He may even use passive preachers, who themselves are afraid to fight, to deceive you.

He convinces these preachers that it is fine to be radical when you were serving Satan, but now that you are serving God, you should be passive, frail, fearful, faintish, scared, fragile, nervous, lonely, doubtful, poor, broke, stressed, malnourished, sickly, defeated and most of all, ready to die. These are all demonic, destructive lies from the pit of hell.

Paul was fully aware of the constant onslaught of these satanic missiles and wrote that even though we live in a natural or fleshly world, this realm is not where the war takes place.

In his contiguous writing, he emphasized the fact that if you believed for one moment that this war is carnal, then you are dead already; but if you understand that it is spiritual, then you will live longer, having an abundant life filled with peace. This peace comes from the confidence in knowing that, *"No weapon formed against you shall prosper,..." (Isaiah 54:17)*

I often equate this "peace" to a man standing in front of his enemy, wearing a bullet proof vest beneath his clothes. The enemy is not aware that the vest is there. So with the only opportunity he has, he fires at the man aiming for his heart. The man stands there boldly because he knows he is protected. The enemy on the other hand leaves defeated.

When your heart is protected by faith and confidence, the only thing left for you to do is fight like a good soldier defeating the enemy. Paul admonishes Timothy to, *"Fight the good fight of faith,..." (1 Timothy 6:12) "...and endure hardness as a good soldier..." (2 Timothy 2:3)*

He uses many military words throughout his writings because he knew that right after his Damascus road experience, he would become the most wanted man in hell and the most misunderstood man in the church. Prior to his conversion, Paul was a wealthy, educated, and popular man who heavily persecuted the believers.

However, none of the above disqualified him from being shot at by satan's army after becoming a Christian. In fact, on many occasions Paul lived like a fugitive - being whipped, shipwrecked, bitten by snakes, let down a huge wall in a basket, stoned, cold, hungry and imprisoned.

After all Paul had gone through, he was still able to write back to the churches to encourage them. He said, *"Finally, my brethren, be strong in the Lord, and in the power of his might."* He went on to say, *"Put on the whole armor of God that you may be able to stand against the wiles of the devil." (Ephesians 6:10-11)*

- *To stand* means to hold or stay your position; not to crumble, falter, or fail in your moment of testing.

- *Against* is another military word which signifies that you are not with the enemy, but are in direct combat or opposition to them.

- *The "wiles of the devil"* represents the plots, plans, strategies that satan has set up in an attempt to destroy you. The wiles further represent the arrows or missiles he has set to be hurled against your anointing.

SATAN'S HIERARCHY

In *2 Corinthians 2:11* we are reminded not to be ignorant concerning Satan's devices lest he would have an advantage over us. As believers, we should know what the will of God is concerning us. It would be very interesting to note that satan's kingdom is organized and he has established a demonic hierarchy which operates under his commands.

Every unclean spirit knows his rank, position, delegated authority and power in the kingdom of darkness. The question is, "Do believers know theirs?" According to *Ephesians 6:12:*

> *"...we do not wrestle against flesh and blood*
> *but against principalities, against powers,*
> *against the rulers of the darkness of this*
> *world, against spiritual wickedness in high*
> *places."*

When you open your mouth to speak or pray, there are two surveillance towers or D.S.S. systems that can pick up your spoken thoughts: either Demonic Satanic Surveillance or Deliverance Spiritual Surveillance. *(See more in Chapter on Spiritual Surveillance vs Satanic Surveillance)*

When you pray negative words of fear and doubt, demonic *principalities* pick them up on their "satellites" and radars. They then transmit these negative signals to the "Powers that be". The *powers*, which are the second highest-ranking demons, activate their laws to the ruling agents called *"the rulers of the darkness of this world."*

As their name suggests, they immediately seek to rule by initiating and activating the consequences of the laws of sin and death. As you continue to succumb to surges of shock waves coming from high voltages of negative influences, you may find yourself weakened in your mind. Demonic strongholds on your mind work with *"spiritual wickedness in high places."* If you allow them, it is then and only then, that witches and warlocks can seek to bring harm to you.

For decades Satan has had Christians praying ignorantly and fighting amongst each other. Instead of declaring war against him and his fallen angels, we have been fighting against each other. It is very important that you understand that this battle is not against flesh and blood. It is not against your spouse, boss, next-door neighbor or children, neither against your mother-in-law.

What you must clearly understand and remember is that this war is *against principalities, against powers, against the rulers of the darkness of this world, against spiritual wickedness in high places.*

Principalities

Principalities are the principal, ruling or reigning order in the kingdom of darkness. Even as its very definition denotes, it is the foundation or basis on which principles are established. *Prince -* being the one chosen and set up to reign or lord over a particular region or kingdom. This "order" is authorized to control and manipulate all who fall under its jurisdiction and as long as they are citizens of that province, they are subject to comply and obey. This, of course, is the case in Monarchies. Once the rulers are set in place the only way they are broken is if a higher power intervenes, invades, bombards and overthrows that existing principality.

This was evident in the life of Daniel as indicated in *Daniel 10:12-13* when the Bible records that Daniel prayed and fasted concerning a matter for twenty-one days. However the prince of Persia that reigned in the spirit of darkness over that area had held captive a "weaker" angel that was sent to deliver the message. It was quite obvious that this prince ruled over the Persian region and held captive the angel that was coming with answers. God, knowing order, sent Michael the Archangel, who was more powerful than this prince to overthrow him, thus releasing Daniel's answer.

Powers

The *Powers* are the executing spirits. The principles or mandates have been set up. It is now the responsibility of the powers to carry them out. Powers only act on instructions, working closely with the *rulers of the darkness of this world*.

For example, if you believe you are sick then they ensure that you become sick by employing the spirits of affliction and infirmity. If you believe that you are poor, they activate the laws that relate to the spirit of poverty to attack your life.

Powers ensure that whatever law is activated through sin and broken covenant, that the curse or penalty for that is issued. Laws are written and set up in a country. If you break them, you suffer the consequences. If you commit a crime, the policeman will stop you, investigate or even arrest you.

It now becomes the decision of the court judge, jury or law as written on the books, what your penalty should be. The verdict is handed down and the law enforcement officers (police or prison officers) issue your penalty(ies) which must be enforced except there is an intervention by a higher order *(Court of Appeal, Privy Council, Supreme Court, House of Parliament, and others)*

The Rulers Of The Darkness Of This World

The rulers of the darkness of this world are territorial demonic spirits that are responsible for keeping the peoples of the world in spiritual darkness. Spiritual *darkness* is a mindset, attitude or disposition of a person devoid of *light.* The Word of God declares that God is light and in Him there is no darkness at all. Therefore these high-ranking demonic spirits work to keep the people of the world ignorant to and devoid of the knowledge of who God is.

These spirits operate through ungodly systems *(systems that do not promote the will, purposes, plan of God),* to distort nations, cities, countries, churches, and individuals' thoughts, feelings, attitudes, behaviors, and mindset such as the media, such as television, radio, magazines, movies, fashion, sports, and other religious dogma.

Spiritual Wickedness in High Places

Spiritual Wickedness in High Places is one of the lowest ranking demons in the satanic kingdom. These demonic forces gain strength by attacking one of the highest points on a man's body, which is his mind. These are also demon spirits which influence witches, warlocks, sorcerers, and voodoo priests.

The spirits that work in spiritual wickedness often lure their candidates, who are sometimes people of status and authority into feeling a sense of invincibility; thinking that they are unreachable and untouchable.

These spirits mesmerize their victims into somewhat of a false sense of power. They believe that they will rule forever and that no one will ever find them out. Most people who operate under this influence, function under the Machiavelli spirit. These people become possessed by ancient demon spirits that use various crafts and diabolical plots to affect people's minds, altering their will and emotions.

THE WHOLE ARMOUR

"Put on the whole armour of God that you may be able to stand against the wiles of the devil." (Ephesians 6:11)

Since we are living in the last days, it is incumbent upon each believer to put on the whole armour of God. Having on the whole armour protects you from the wiles of the devil and equips you for spiritual warfare.

You cannot go to a fight unless you are dressed right. God gives us a spiritual dress code that we must all wear daily.

Your spiritual armour includes the following:
1. *The Helmet of Salvation* – you must be born again. The helmet protects your head which is your mind. Satan will try to attack your mind to destroy you.

2. *The Breastplate of Righteousness* – holy character and moral conduct. The breastplate protects the most critical area, which is your heart.

    "It is with the heart one believes unto righteousness." (Romans 10:10)

    "... the righteous are as bold as a lion." (Proverbs 28:1)
    "Keep (guard) your heart with all diligence, for out of it are the issues of life." (Proverbs 4:23)

3. *The Shield of Faith* – utmost confidence and trust in God. This shield was used to protect the entire body,

soul and spirit from Satan's devices and extinguishes the fiery darts of the enemy.

4. *The Sword of the Spirit* – the Word of God. Study to show yourself approved unto God. Rhema, in the Greek, means the spoken Word. The Word of God is one of the most powerful weapons against the enemy.

5. *The Girdle of Truth* - living with integrity and honesty.

6. *Feet shod with Preparation of the Gospel of Peace – "Thy word is a lamp unto my feet, and a light unto my path." (Psalm 119:105)* Shoes represent your ability. Thus, you must be willing to take the Word of God everywhere you go in a spirit of peace and love.

7. *All Prayer and Supplication – "The effectual fervent prayer of the righteous man availeth much." (James 5:16b)* Prayer is another very powerful weapon against the enemy if aimed properly. *(See more in Chapter 19 on Militant Prayer)*

W.O.M.B.: WEAPONS OF MASSIVE BREAKTHROUGH

As a believer, now that you have gone through the Dimensions of Worship and know who you are in Christ Jesus, you should have sweatless victories in your everyday life. It is not God's will that you spend every second of the day fighting demons. However, because you may constantly encounter the enemy, you should be equipped to disarm and destroy his arsenals.

It is very important to understand that, *"For though we walk in the flesh, we do not war after the flesh." (2 Corinthians 10:3)* There must come a time in your life when you put the devil to flight. As Christians we spend most of our days crying and pleading with the devil to leave us alone.

As soldiers we must know when and where to cry. Furthermore, we must know how to recover when life pulls the floor from beneath us.

"Behold, I have given unto you power (authority) over all the powers (abilities, tactics or plans) of the enemy.
(Luke 10:19 AMP)

You must begin to use your *Weapons Of Massive Breakthrough* (**W.O.M.B.**) and without fear or failure defeat the devil. Some of these weapons of mass destruction are: prayer, praise, worship, laying prostrate, walking and stomping, dancing, fasting, faith, the Word, and giving an offering.

In the book of Joel, chapters 2 and 3, God declares Himself as a God of war (Jehovah Gibhor). In *Joel 3:10,* He encourages us to beat our plowshares into spears and our pruning hooks into swords. *It's War Time!*

In other words, God is saying that there is no time to waste digging up in the dirt. Just as we use tools to till the ground to reap a harvest, we must use spiritual tools Weapons Of Massive Breakthrough (W.O.M.B.), to till and defeat the plans of the enemy.

Further, in *2 Corinthians 10:4* the Word of God says that *"the weapons of our warfare are not carnal,..."* meaning that this war is not one where physical guns and grenades, or anything else that we can see, are used, but that our weapons are mighty through God to the pulling down of strongholds.

This means that our weapons are powerfully attainable through our faith in God and we become equipped to bring down any hiding place the devil seeks to set up, even in our minds. Remember this is a spiritual fight and the battle generally begins in the mind.

Paul emphasizes the fact that even though we walk (live) in the flesh or this natural body, the war that we are fighting is not a fleshly one, it is a spiritual one. This means that we are fighting an enemy that lives in an invisible realm. This archenemy has become the master of his tricks and schemes.

Paul further admonishes us that we should not be ignorant of satan's devices *(2 Corinthians 2:11)*. God says His people are destroyed for a lack of knowledge. In *Daniel 11:32* the prophet writes that "...*the people that do know their God shall be strong, and do exploits.*"

CHAPTER TEN

~∽⊗⟨⊙⟩⊗∽~

BEWARE OF THE SPIRIT OF WITCHCRAFT

WITCHCRAFT

Witchcraft, in various historical and religious contexts is the use of certain kinds of supernatural or magical powers in an effort to manipulate or control people. People who are involved in such practices, may also seek to use their demonic powers to manipulate the outcome of various events. Further, whenever someone seeks to use incantations, potions or powders to control another person's life, they are practicing a form of witchcraft. A witch is someone who engages in these and other demonic or occult practices.

Today a modern male practitioner of witchcraft, especially in Wicca may also be called a witch, although frequently known as a warlock. This term was considered offensive because the origin of the word meant "truth" (waer) and "misrepresenter" (logere) translated "truth misrepresenter" or "faith breaker."

Witchcraft is the manipulation and control of an individual's mind.   Once you are able to control an individual's mind, you are able to control their life. There are various forms of witchcraft which may involve Santeria, sorcery, white magic and black magic, which involve forms of spellcrafts, jinxcrafts, incantations, hexes, dolls, crosses, candles, graveyard dirt, powders, potions, Ouija boards, tarot cards, all affiliations and such like.

Demonic spirits, through these mediums, seek to inflict terror and torture in the lives of individuals who fall prey to their deceptive practices. Voodoo, a form of witchcraft, involves live sacrifices, including animals, birds, human life, and others.

Throughout the course of my ministry, many people have come seeking healing and deliverance from ailments, sicknesses and diseases. In some cases, many people spend much time and money with their medical physicians and psychologists seeking help only to discover that the symptoms of these ailments were not physical but were attacks from the demonic spirit realm.

Many churches are also under diabolical witchcraft attacks. Some pastors have not been able to advance because of these attacks and many have even given up on the call of God for their lives.

In other cases there are some unexplainable turns of events. Many pastors are unable to understand why their church may not be growing or why half of their once united congregation has left in a "ball of confusion." Many pastors and people have been derailed out of the will of God because of these attacks.

In most cases the individual expends much needed energies, gifts, talents, abilities, and anointing trying to get back into and fulfill the perfect will of God for their lives and in some cases may never do so.

Some believers are afraid of people who seem to possess these demonic powers. Not realizing that we, as Christians possess more spiritual authority through Jesus Christ than witches, warlocks, soothsayers, crystal readers, stargazers or necromancers put together. These wicked demons use the spirits of fear, doubt and intimidation to torment, torture and lure their victims into a state of panic, eventually overpowering their soul.

You must all remember that God has given you total authority over evil spirits, including the spiritually wicked ones that dwell in "high places."

In *1 Peter 5:8* it states that *satan is as a roaring lion seeking whom he may devour.* "As" is a simile meaning that he is not a lion. He just walks around growling at believers, to see their response. If you respond in a manner that suggests fear or unbelief in God our Father, then he moves in for the kill. Witchcraft cannot overpower you unless you allow it to do so.

> *"...greater is He that is in you, than he that is in the world." (1 John 4:4)*

In some instances, the weapons may be formed but they cannot prosper. You may be a little afflicted but not infected. Many Christians have been found guilty of practicing witchcraft. Even seeking counsel from them witches, soothsayers, and the like makes you accountable. If you have ever consulted with a witch or palm reader, you should immediately repent and break every curse that may have come over your life or the life of your children.

> In *Exodus 22:18*, it says, *"Thou shall not suffer a witch to live."*

Soothsayers, palm-readers, magicians, and witches defy the Word of God and twist it to bring about evil ambitions. God has always severely punished the witch and even those who consult with them.

In our world today, many people, including some churches have tolerated and accepted the practice of witchcraft as culture and seek to justify it validity. Remember, God issued a firm warning to the church of Thyatira for allowing the spirit of witchcraft to operate and that death shall come to all who practice such things.

> *"But the fearful, and unbelieving, and the abominable, and murderers, and whoremongers, and sorcerers, and idolaters, and all liars, shall have their part in the lake which burneth with fire and brimstone: which is the second death." (Revelation 21:8)*

CHARISMATIC WITCHCRAFT

Charismatic witchcraft is manipulation from the pulpit or the seat of authority that seeks to undermine followers to do or believe things that are contrary to the Word of God.

Many political leaders use charismatic witchcraft in their speeches and writings; making vain campaign promises in order to win the vote of the masses. However, when these people are elected to positions of power, they conveniently forget the promises made during their election campaign and only use their power for personal gain.

In other instances, some political leaders being used by ungodly influences seek to legislate laws that are designed to draw the hearts and minds of the people away from God. This sometimes subtle strategy of the enemy is conveniently camouflaged in political rhetoric which deceptively states that it seeks the "good of all people."

Some leaders may use the spirit of religion to ensnare people into legalism and idolatry. One of the attributes of this legalistic spirit is the rigid practice of certain doctrines, beliefs, ideologies or procedures due to the influences of various cultures or upbringings.

As a leader, you must always remember that the mandate upon your life is to teach the Word of God. In spite of what is going on around you, God is counting on you to always preach *"that which becomes sound doctrine."*

WITCHCRAFT FROM THE PEWS

In today's modern day church, where people have become more knowledgeable and empowered, they have now taken their new sense of power to the extreme and are now trying to manipulate and control what is preached from the pulpit.

Some members use the spirit of influence and wealth to dictate how the church should be run. This is witchcraft and should not, under any circumstances, be tolerated by leaders. Business owners should also be aware of this same spirit that may seek to work through employees or unionized members of their establishment.

The spirit of witchcraft is another manifestation of the spirit of Jezebel and can sometimes be seen in subtle body gestures as the man of God is speaking or the Word is being preached. Such gestures may include: the rolling of the eyes, the folding of the arms while seated, the shake of the head in strong disapproval of what was said, and many others. The withholding of tithes and offerings is another tactic used by "pew witches" to destroy churches.

Other examples are demonized boards and auxiliaries filled with unregenerated, "power hungry" individuals seeking to dictate and usurp the authority of the pastor, with every intention of fulfilling their own purposes. The church should be run "Theocratically", this is, God to the Pastor, and not democratically, that is God, the pastor, the board and the pew.

In the midst of all of this confusion, it is impossible for the power or the presence of God to manifest in the service. The Word of God declares that light and darkness have no fellowship. Further, the Word states that God is light and in Him there is no darkness at all. If we choose to live in darkness, confusion, and contention, God cannot move. He will not force Himself in an atmosphere where He is not wanted nor welcomed. If we allow the spirit of Jezebel, witchcraft, confusion, and contention to remain, then the Spirit, the presence and the glory of God will leave.

BEWARE OF JEZEBEL
(Witchcraft, Mayhem, Anarchy, Deception)

The spirit of Jezebel is an ancient principality spirit that has for centuries destroyed families, governments, businesses and yes, even great churches. She is a goddess of war. The name Jezebel means unmarried or unhusbanded and seeks to do just that. This manipulating, subtly destructive spirit, seeks to keep those she has under her control disloyal and unsubmitted to authority.

Even though *1 Kings 18* speaks of the woman Jezebel, you should understand that this is a spirit and does not necessarily have anything to do with being a woman. It can operate through a male or female. The Hebrews refers to her as the "priest of Baal" with abilities to influence both genders.

The spirit of Jezebel dislikes divine order, holiness and cannot stand the prophetic anointing. The spirit of Jezebel always wants to be in charge and will undermine the existing protocol through rebellion, manipulation and subliminal control.

"For rebellion is as the sin of witchcraft, and stubbornness is as iniquity and idolatry ..."
(1 Samuel 15:23)

Every prophetic warrior must fight against the spirit of Jezebel. If you do not defeat her, she will do her utmost best to defeat you. The spirit of Jezebel will either disguise herself as a prophet brewing lies, confusion and witchcraft, or she will outrightly attack those that have a prophetic anointing.

Many people who are called by God with a prophetic mantle have, at some point, experienced Jezebelic manifestations in their lives. You see, Jezebel knows if she cannot beat you, it is better that she joins you and take full control of your mind.

Thus, she loves the prophet who is puffed up in pride and who goes after the money more than God, as Balaam the prophet did in the book of Numbers. She loves the secretary who is anointed but loves to gossip. She makes independent business owners haughty and arrogant, deceiving them into believing that all they have accomplished was as a result of their own strength, intelligence and "business savvy" and not because of the grace of God.

The spirit of Jezebel loves weak, unfaithful husbands who are married to unsubmitted, contentious and argumentative wives. She sits back as total chaos and confusion wreck their lives.

She adores wicked politicians who use their political powers for filthy and personal gain. She allows them to implement laws that are immoral and that will bring entire Nations under curses.

She loves armourbearers who are opportunists only serving their leader but want their own power, as with the account recorded in *2 Samuel 15:1-6* about Absalom.

This spirit seeks to take over the mind and will of an individual. Her ultimate plan is to subvert the believer from ever fulfilling God's divine will. In *Revelation 2:18-24* the church at Thyatira was rebuked for tolerating the spirit of Jezebel and for allowing her to operate as a false prophet.

The spirit of Jezebel can manifest as a false prophet in some of the following ways:

Erroneous teachings	*False Doctrines*
Heresy	*Spiritual Adultery*
Spiritual Fornication	*Compromise*
Mind Control	*Spirit of Religion*
Arrogance	*Imitated Anointing*
Spirit of Rebellion	*and much more*

Today, many pastors, churches, and members tolerate or allow the spirit of Jezebel to reign in their lives and congregations. She is contentious and confrontational. Even though she can stand alone, at times she will use the spirit of Ahab to help carry out her diabolical assignments. *(1 Kings 16:33)*

Jezebel has many strongmen working to advance her agenda, one of these is pride and the other is perversion.

"Pride goes before destruction and an haughty spirit before a fall." (Proverbs 16:18)

Pride

The spirit of Pride is a strongman that works under the Spirit of Jezebel. This spirit causes you to become high minded, boastful and seeks to gain glory unto itself. Satan has established his kingdom on the spirit of pride, and even thought of himself more highly than of God, thus he and one third of the angels were cast out of heaven.

When you are operating in the spirit of pride, you are not working according to the Kingdom of God, but according to a satanic mindset. Pride is self-conceited and full of vainglory.

Pride manifests itself in a myriad of ways such as:

Self-gratification	False submission
Self-righteousness	Independence
Haughtiness	Strife
Offense	Rebellion
Hatred	Vanity
False Humility	Disobedience
Manipulation	Egotism
Control	High-mindedness
Unteachableness	Disrespect
Arrogance	Jealousy
Exaggeration	and much more.

Growing up, we were taught to have pride in ourselves. However, it is when we operate in the spirit of pride that we cause harm to others rather than good. This is not the will of God concerning us.

Perversion

Jezebel also works with a strongman called perversion and can manifest through sexual perversion, spiritual perversion or even financial perversion. The word perversion means to be "twisted." Thus, Jezebel through perversion seeks to twist everything from the right way to the wrong way.

Sexual Perversion can be characterized by:

Lewd Lust/Conduct	Inordinate affections
Fornication	Bestiality
Masturbation	Homosexuality
Adultery	Lesbianism
Oral Sex	Incest
Anal sex	Rape
Pedophilia	Molestation
Pornography	Sex while menstruating
Orgies	Prostitution
Transvestitism	and much more

Spiritual Perversion can be characterized by:
Heresies
Baal/Idol Worship
Charismatic Witchcraft
Mind Control
False Doctrines of man and devils

Financial Perversion can be characterized by:
Extortion
Gambling
Illegal Gain
Filthy Lucre – illegal gains

Sexual perversion is sweeping through the corridors of homes, schools, and churches. Jezebel conspires with other demonic spirits releasing poisonous venoms which destroy ministries, marriages, corporations and countless lives. *We must fight to bring Jezebel down!*

God is raising up true Apostles and Prophets that are going to throw down the spirit of Jezebel and her false teachings without fear or failure.

In *1 Kings 21:23* God raised up Elijah to prophesy the demise of Jezebel the Queen and later raised up Jehu to bring her down. To gain total victory over this spirit, you must expose, dismantle, and destroy her plans, altars of Baal *(or false doctrines)* and all of her children, especially Athaliah.

The impending Apostolic-Prophetic move of God is going to usher in a revival predicated by "holy fire" that will not be manipulated, quenched or stopped by any demonic spirit.

Demonic spirits of Jezebel, Ahab, Pharaoh, Herod, and Egypt which had the people of God in bondage will no longer be able to prevail or hinder what God is getting ready to do in the earth realm.

THE SPIRIT OF AHAB

The spirit of Ahab is a co-dependent spirit that works directly with the spirit of Jezebel. This spirit attacks people, causing them to become fearful of rejection. Further individuals under the influence of this spirit tend to neglect their authoritative position, do no assume responsibility for their actions and are chronic complainers. This spirit subtly appears to be weak and, for the most part, is irresponsible.

Some of the characteristics of the spirit of Ahab are:

Intimidation	*Memory loss*
Procrastination	*Perversion*
Disorganization	*Hidden Agendas*
Slothfulness	*Laziness*
Argumentative	*Ungrateful*
Provoking	

In the book of *1 Kings 16:30-33* it speaks of King Ahab. The bible says that he provoked God to anger more than all the kings of Israel that were before him. It was Ahab that built the altar of Baal and worshipped him. He was wicked, rebellious and self-conceited. Do not tolerate this spirit in your life; dethrone it in Jesus' name.

THE COCKATRICE EGGS

Have you ever wondered as a pastor how, generally, right after a mighty move of God in your church that confusion and contention break out and people leave?

This happens because the spirit of Jezebel is at work within the congregation. This controlling spirit always wants to have her own way; if she cannot; she leaves, taking with her innocent, weak church members who had similar "eggs hatching in them."

This spirit of the cockatrice works for Jezebel like a snake laying thousands of eggs and can be likened to bad seeds of jealousy, envy, strife, and rebellion. It knits subtle, almost invisible webs forming "cliques", alliances, allegiances or soul ties with others of the same mindset through the spirit of affinity.

Once in place the conspiracy begins, normally by attacking the leader or true prophetic voice, by spreading erroneous lies or by simply disagreeing with everything the leader wants to do. This also happens in businesses or even in the workplace. The individuals laying the eggs may sometimes be family members, friends, or even co-workers. They send demonic spirits to attack the person closest to the prophet, pastor or manager so that there is always confusion between the leader and their close subordinates, such as armourbearers, secretaries and other people serving in the Church.

At times, overwhelmed and frustrated, the leader may remove his aid. Jezebel then takes this opportunity to replace that person with someone else who is carrying more of her eggs, insinuating that they are able to do the job better.

Bear in mind, Jezebel wants full authority and will use this cockatrice spirit to knit a web of confusion to ensnare and trap those who fall victim to her subtle workings. In *Isaiah 59:2-3, 5-8* the prophet warns about the cockatrice spirit:

> [2]*"...your iniquities have separated between you and your God, and your sins have hid His face from you, that He will not hear."*

> [3]*"For your hands are defiled with blood, and your fingers with iniquity; your lips have spoken lies, your tongue hath uttered perverseness."*

> [5]*"They hatch cockatrice' eggs, and weave the spider's web: he that eateth of their eggs dieth, and that which is crushed breaketh out into a viper."*

> [6]*"Their webs shall not become garments, neither shall they cover themselves with their works: their works are works of iniquity, and the act of violence is in their hands."*

> [7]*"Their feet run to evil, and they make haste to shed innocent blood: their thoughts are thoughts of iniquity; wasting and destruction are in their paths."*

> [8]*"The way of peace they know not; and there is no judgment in their goings: they have made them crooked paths: whosoever goeth therein shall not know peace."*

This spirit works in alignment with other demonic spirits. If this demonized dynasty is not carefully and properly dismantled you may almost lose an entire congregation, business, marriage or even your own life.

THE SPIRIT OF RELIGION

The spirit of religion is a spirit that operates by being highly devoted to religious activities such as, serving on the usher board or in the hospitality ministry, and other areas. This spirit causes an individual to spend more time focusing on religious practices and religious dogma more so than cultivating an intimate relationship with God through prayer and study of the Word, fasting and corporate worship.

Individuals operating in a spirit of religion are more susceptible to operating in a spirit of Jezebel. The spirit of Jezebel is very attracted to religious people who are more devoted to religious activities more than they are devoted to a relationship with God.

These people are excited about Church but want nothing to do with the Kingdom of God. They are comfortable with activities such as serving on the church board, attending church fairs, picnics and events but are unavailable for times of Bible study, corporate prayer and fasting. In some cases, these people are not willing to give their tithe to the local church but are willing to purchase items they believe the church needs.

They may even operate under the disguise of false prophetic or false evangelistic anointing.

*The spirit of religion can manifest in several ways;
through or by the following:*

Pride	Hypocrisy
Unteachableness	Arrogance
Blasphemy	Idolatry
Unbelief	Irreverence
Divisiveness	Self-Righteousness
Deception	Controlling
Manipulation	Judgmental

You must bind the spirit of religion and loose it from its assignment. Declare the Word of God and release the spirit of truth, disarming demonic spirits and forbidding them to operate.

CHURCH SPLITS

Many churches have been formed by people acting in a spirit of rebellion or disagreement. Most of these churches break away from a "parent church" in total chaos and disorder, sometimes tearing the very souls of their leaders. Jezebel boasts of her success in many church splits as she does in business splits.

"Can two walk together, except they agree?"
(Amos 3:3)

This is not the way God ordained it to be. In most cases they may start out appearing to be blessed, but in reality, they are not. Unless these "break away" churches and leaders repent, they will continue to experience brewing contentions and unholy wars in their newly formed church.

*"God is looking for true servants and not
bastards."*

BEWARE OF SEDUCING SPIRITS

In some instances, many once faithful sons and daughters in ministry have been deceived by seducing spirits. To seduce means more than being enticed in a relationship with someone of the opposite sex.   In this context, *to seduce* means to lure or entice away from responsibilities, principles, godly conduct or service with a promise or suggestion of offering something better.

Many people in the Body of Christ truly love God and love their Pastors. However, after a period of faithful service, as in the case of Demas who left the Apostle Paul *(2 Timothy 4:10)*, they were seduced away from their kingdom assignment due to the cares of this life.

In *Matthew 13:22*, the Bible warns that these cares can literally choke out, or better, causes an individual to completely forget the Word that they themselves once received. They literally forget promises to God and promises they made to loyally serve their Pastors and complete their kingdom assignment.

In other instances, some people have been so deceived by the enemy that they are convinced and seek to convince others that, by separating from their Pastors and their local Church that they are on a special mission *for* God. Those who walk closely with their Leaders must be careful not to be entrapped by seducing spirits which are released over the Body of Christ to bring separation and confusion. They may erroneously believe that their desire to "break away" is actually God calling them to establish another "work" separate from what He has called their Pastors to.

God is a God of order. He will not impress upon you to leave your spiritual mother and father unless He has spoken to them and they are in agreement. I believe that as you faithfully serve a man or woman of God your gift will make room for you. In the right time, it will set you before kings and mighty men. If God is truly calling you to pastor a church or preach the Gospel, I believe that it will be with the full understanding, approval and blessing of your leader.

God, Himself, ordained succession. Elisha was anointed to succeed Elijah. Ruth needed a Naomi to get her to her blessed place. Even John the Baptist baptized Jesus in the river Jordan which heralded His earthly ministry. There was neither competition nor contention in the midst of these great men and women of God; as one came on the scene the other faded because the idea of succession was understood.

However, not every instance of succession or mentorship functioned as well as the others mentioned above. In the case of King Saul and David, his successor, a spirit of jealousy, envy, rebellion and disobedience had overcome King Saul. There were many instances where Saul tried to kill David.

Many opportunities were presented to David where he could have retaliated and killed Saul. In *1 Samuel 26:9*, it is recorded where such an opportunity presented itself to David. He was faster than Saul, he had already killed more enemies of the Israel than Saul and had already been ordained by the prophet Samuel, but yet he refused to kill Saul.

"...Touch not mine anointed and do my prophets no harm." (1 Chronicles 16:22)

If you are serving under a leader with a "Saul-like spirit", pray and allow God himself to deal with that person and just wait on your appointed time, I guarantee you it will come. When it became difficult for Paul and Barnabas to remain on the same assignment, God separated them for the sake of the ministry. Similarly, when Lot's herdsmen fought with Abraham's herdsmen the Lord separated them also. This spirit usually overwhelms an individual and causes them to strive with their spiritual leader or some other spiritual authority.

"Do not destroy another man's vineyard or later someone else will come and destroy yours."

The spirit of Jezebel can manifest in your life, ministry and workplace in some of the following ways:

Anarchy	Jealousy
Competition	Violence
Deception	Hatred of Authority
Rebellion	Manipulation
Contention/Strife	Blasphemy
Slander/Lies	Unsubmissiveness
Retaliation	Envy
Insubordination	Idolatry
Anger/Hatred	Fear/Intimidation
Vanity	Blatant persecution
Irreverence	Lewd Affections
Manipulation/Control	Confrontation
Isolation	Warring spirit
Greed For Power	Sabotage
	and more.

THE ZODIAC

Satan has astro-demon spirits which work and maneuver through astrology and the signs of the Zodiac. These astro-demons give *their mediums, psychics, soothsayers, and the like,* powers from a demonic realm in order to carry out various functions. These psychics have different deities, gods and goddesses which they worship through the sun, moon, and stars.

Many of them practice levitation *(the lifting of one's body or objects by the power of the mind)*, astro-projections *(movement of the spirit out of the body)*, metaphysics *(mind over matter–controlling the physical realm using your mind)* and are faithful to reading and believing their daily horoscopes.

One of the greatest strategies of the enemy is to seek to imitate or pervert all that is God or that has been created by Him. The Bible clearly states that satan is able to transform himself *as* an angel of light. Satan, the great deceiver, imitator, and copycat can only pervert or mimic that which is holy, right, and true. His kingdom is the exact antithesis to the kingdom of God.

The signs of the zodiac have a true presence in the night sky. Many people can point out the constellation of stars that make up Orion, The "Bear", The Big and Little Dipper and others. Many astronomers have researched the stars and have uncovered great mysteries that were hidden in them.

However, just as with everything that God has created, He warns us never to worship the creature, or the creation, *more* than the Creator. *(Romans 1:25)*

Many believers are more dedicated to reading their daily horoscope and following astrological charts seeking answers about their mates, "divine" connections, business opportunities and the like than seeking answers from God. You should not worship the signs nor seek answers concerning your destiny from them. Opening these doors may invite a demonic presence into your home and may prove fatal.

The Word of God is very clear in *Isaiah 47:13-14* which states that stargazers, monthly prognosticators, sorcerers and astrologers will be judged with fire. It further states that

"...they shall not deliver themselves from the power of the flame..."

The signs of the zodiac have been perverted from their original purpose. These symbols were originally used to forever unveil the message of the gospel, depicting a conquering Christ but have now been twisted and taken by the world as signs and symbols of idolatry and idol worship.

When seeking answers, many people usually turn to palm-readers, crystal gazers, sooth-sayers, their daily horoscopes and signs of the zodiac such as:

Virgo	*Libra*
Scorpio	*Aquarius*
Sagittarius	*Pisces*
Capricorn	*Gemini*
Cancer	*Leo*
Taurus	*Aries*

Although the signs and symbols were placed in the heavens to point mankind to the redemptive plan of God, it is worth repeating and emphasizing that God did not intend for us to worship the stars, the sun, the moon, or any of His creation for that matter.

Other forms of the occult also seek answers through the assistance of familiar spirits through some of these signs. These craft-workers may also seek to communicate with the dead, which is known as necromancy.

Some may even use numbers, symbols, and forms of ritualistic arts such as chanting, dancing, and even sacrifices (animal or human) to invoke evil power from these demonic and familiar spirits.

According to *Deuteronomy 18:9-14*, such practices are an abomination unto the Lord. It is important to understand, however, that we were created to worship. If we do not worship God, we will worship something or someone else. God created us so that we could worship Him and Him alone.

CHAPTER ELEVEN

SPIRITUAL SURVEILLANCE VS. SATANIC SURVEILLANCE

PROPHETIC SPIRITUAL SURVEILLANCES

The office of the Prophet, along with the prophetic giftings in the Body of Christ, is given to break chains and demonic strongholds off of the lives of those who are bound. The prophetic watchman has been equipped with spiritual surveillance devices for the kingdom of God. Prior to satan ever set up his Demonic Satanic Surveillance (DSS), God had already established His Deliverance Spiritual Surveillance (DSS). Remember, the enemy only twists or imitates what God has already done.

Without this Deliverance Spiritual Surveillance (DSS) system in place the body of Christ may experience brutal attacks and encounter many casualties.

However, just as there are different ranks and officers of spiritual surveillance in the kingdom of God – satan also has different ranks and principalities.

For example, whenever a believer becomes offended when rebuked by their leader, through the preached or taught Word of God, they may begin to feel as though the person ministering is targeting them. If this person rejects or disagrees with what is being taught, Demonic Satanic, Surveillances (DSS) immediately detect this and release a spirit of offense to build a wall around the individual, which hinders him from receiving the Word.

The Demonic Satanic Surveillances (DSS) immediately transmit signals to other demon spirits, such as anger, resentment and a "wall-out" spirit. Therefore, this small opening created a gateway for more attacks from the kingdom of darkness. In most cases, this once submitted believer leaves the church in total offence and rebellion. This is all a part of Satan's plan to keep individuals in bondage.

Jesus constantly encourages us to watch and pray. In John 6 He warned His disciples about these subtle unercurrents which will seek to beset and turn them away from the kingdom.

In fact, in *Revelation 3:2* the author admonishes us to *"be watchful, and strengthen the things which remain, that are ready to die:..."* In other words, wake up and begin to strengthen yourself in prayer; do not allow the enemy to kill or destroy you or anything that belongs to you.

As a *Prophetic Watchman* God is calling you to sharpen your spiritual perception and like never before stay your position on the wall.

THE PROPHETIC WATCHMAN
"... except the Lord keep the city, the
watchman waketh but in vain."
(Psalm 127:1b)

God is looking for watchmen. Prophetic Watchmen remain on high alert, sounding an alarm to warn the city of ensuing danger. As a prophetic watchman, you have been chosen and ordained by God to infiltrate and bombard the kingdom of darkness. As your name suggests, you, through your spiritual senses are able to discern satanic interference and through powerful spiritual warfare, annihilate and destroy their plans.

As a prophetic intercessor, you must remember that you have been placed on the wall like the Prophet Joel to blow the trumpet in Zion. This trumpet is sounded to alert the kingdom citizens to saddle their horses and pray.

You must walk in a keen seer's anointing with spiritual boldness like Ezekiel, the Prophet, to warn the people in the city of impending dangers ahead. The prophetic watchman is always on the lookout and possesses a keen spirit of discernment.

As a prophetic watchman, your days can be long and strenuous at times. You are sometimes the last to go to sleep and usually the first to wake up. Prophetic Watchmen with spiritual surveillance abilities may include, but are not limited to:

- Prophets
- Prophetic Seers
- Prophetic Dreamers
- Prophetic Intercessors
- Prophetic Prayer Warriors

Prophetic Intercessors and Prayer Warriors are spiritual gatekeepers. They act somewhat like the white blood cells in our bodies. Once a signal has been sent to the brain that there is an infection somewhere, thousands of these blood cells rush to that area to protect and fight off the agents causing the infection. This is evident whenever you may receive a minor bruise or cut on your skin. After a few days, you may notice a "scab" forming on the surface of your skin to protect it.

Prophetic Intercessors and *Prophetic Prayer Warriors* do not just pray the problem, they pray the solution. Prophetic Intercessors make bold declarations and walk in strategic alignment with the divine will of God.

These anointed ambassadors pray in accordance with God's Word, His Divine will and purpose. As the name suggests, Intercessors are empowered by the Holy Spirit with the ability to stand in between the problem and activate the solution. They are mandated by God to stand in the gap and make up the hedge. *(Ezekiel 22:30)*

PROPHETIC DREAMERS
"And it shall come to pass afterward, that I will pour out my spirit upon all flesh; and your sons and your daughters shall prophesy, your old men shall dream dreams, your young men shall see visions." (Joel 2:28)

In the Body of Christ, Prophetic Dreamers are very important. God has granted them a gifted ability to fall asleep and dream of profound things which are to come. Dreamers must live a consecrated life being careful to keep their eye and ear gates clean, as this area of gifting can easily become contaminated.

You must be very careful of what you say or allow to come into your soul's "gateways" (ie. Mind, eyes, ears, mouth, nose, pores). Further, you must be mindful of what you watch on television and shield yourself from horror or satanically powered movies. Dreams involve the subconscious aspect of the soul. If this area of your life becomes crowded, contaminated or polluted, this can tamper with the prophetic flow of God in your life, including your dreams. Satan can only gain access if you let him in.

"Keep (guard) your heart with all diligence, for out of it are the issues of life." (Proverbs 4:23)

A dream or vision is a photograph you see in the spirit realm where the Spirit of God reveals to you something that has happened, something that is happening or is about to happen. In the dream realm, whether a "day" dream, night dream or vision you are sometimes required to seek out its interpretation because it may include typologies, colors, symbolisms, numbers etc. For this reason some dreams may have to be interpreted or "unlocked."

Whereas some dreams may need an interpretation, others are very clear and need no interpretation; these are what we may call *visions*. In a vision, you know, beyond the shadow of a doubt what you see. For the most part, they are clear and accurate about what they are intended to convey.

Some prophetic dreamers were Daniel, Jacob, Peter and Joseph. Joseph and Daniel also had the gift of interpreting dreams and helped to change entire nations.

The next dimension of dreamers are those whom, even without falling asleep, can see in the spirit realm, through the gift of faith and revelation. They will begin to see visions of what is happening, what is to come and will not be afraid to see and declare what God has shown them.

125

Once this prophetic watchman picks up dangers or satanic interferences ahead, he transmits a signal to the prophetic intercessors that are on his team and alert them to pray. They may in turn speak with their church leader, Apostle, or Pastor, in most cases, only confirming what God has already shown the Leader. The other ministries in the Church are then informed so that they can all synchronize their gifts and anointings to defeat the enemy and glorify God.

These other areas may include but are not limited to:

- prophetic armour-bearers
- prophetic psalmists
- prophetic teachers
- prophetic ushers
- prophetic administrators
- prophetic congregations

DIVERSITIES OF GIFTS

There are many classifications and diversities of spiritual gifts which are available to you, as a believer. The Spirit of God releases these gifts in your life for His glory. *(1 Corinthians 12:4–10)*

Some of these gifts include, but are not limited to:

- *Word of Wisdom*
- *Word of Knowledge*
- *Gifts of Faith*
- *Gift of Healing*
- *Working of Miracles*
- *Gift of Prophecy*
- *Discerning of spirits*
- *Diverse Tongues*
- *Interpretation of Tongues*

I encourage you even as the Apostle Paul did to covet earnestly the best gifts. In other words, seek God diligently and He will bestow upon you the gift or gifts He so desires.

Some of These Gifts Can Be Placed In Three Basic Categories

- *The Revelatory Gifts* – are the spiritual gifts which include: the word of wisdom, the word of knowledge and the discerning of spirits.
    - *The Word of Wisdom* is divine, supernatural revelation given by God.
    - *The Word of Knowledge* is divine revelation from the mind of God concerning events or situations that may not ordinarily be known.
    - *Discerning of Spirits* is the divine ability to interpret the activity taking place in the spirit realm. It is the "seeing and knowing" of the functions and manifestations of spirits by the Holy Spirit.

- *The Power Gifts* – are the gifts of faith, healing and the working of miracles

- *The Vocal Gifts* – are tongues, interpretation of tongues and the gift of prophecy

There are so many more spiritual gifts that the Spirit of God will give to us which are waiting to be unlocked in the spirit realm. Such gifts include creative miracles and others.

God has anointed you with a divine calling and kingly assignment. The role of kings is to make decrees or declarations, establish laws and defend their domain. Therefore, you must diligently seek the face of God and, as you cultivate the fruit of the spirit in your life, begin to operate in your spiritual gifts, kingdom authority and power.

A Few Other Prophetic Warrior Giftings in The Kingdom Of God are as follows:

- *Prophetic Musicians* – unrehearsed musicians that are able to flow in the Spirit of God, synchronized as one, even with an ability to play music never written before

- *Prophetic Psalmist* – flows in the anointing and sings as the Holy Spirit gives prophetic utterance

- *Prophetic Armourbearers* – shields, protects, and guards the anointing on their leader's life. They help to carry the burden of their leader and ministry, regardless of their needs, by serving perpetually

- *Prophetic Cupbearer* – serves their spiritual leader with a keen spirit of discernment, ensuring that no diabolical plan of the enemy penetrates the anointing. (serving daily and fasting often)

- *Prophetic Dancers* – are divinely anointed to move in a dimension of spiritual exuberance, unimaginable. Every detailed expression is synchronized to tell a message. As the dance may precede a preached word, each individual in the audience should clearly understand what message is being demonstrated at that time. As a prophetic dancer you must live a holy and a clean life before God – even when you spin, what is in your spirit can easily be released onto the congregation whether it is good or bad. It is very important that each believer in the kingdom of God understands the importance of a pure heart.

WALKING IN THE FIVE-FOLD ANOINTING

Jesus walked in an anointing that was very powerful and was visible throughout His entire life.

In Luke 4:18 Jesus said the Spirit of the Lord was upon Him and that He was anointed to do several things:
- To preach the gospel
- To heal the broken-hearted
- To preach deliverance to the captives
- To give recovery of sight to the blind
- To set at liberty them that are bruised
- To preach the acceptable year of the Lord

Jesus was a preacher, teacher, healer, deliverer, and miracle worker walking in an Apostolic-Prophetic mantle. He gave His disciples the same authority and it has been passed on to you. Jesus said:

"... the works that I do shall he do also; and greater works than these shall he do; because I go unto my Father." (John 14:12)

"Behold I give unto you power to tread on serpents and scorpions, and over all the power of the enemy: and nothing shall by any means hurt you." (Luke 10:19)

As a child of God, you must begin to discover where you fit in the kingdom of God and begin walking in that kingly anointing.

PROPHETIC WARRIOR OFFICES IN THE KINGDOM

It is amazing how the Armed Forces, namely the Army, The Navy Seals, The Marines, and Police Forces, have their Commanders-In-Chief, Commodores, and Lieutenants all defined within specific ranks and orders; each officer knowing exactly what they are called to do.

One of the things that I have noticed over the years is that the satanic kingdom also seems to be very organized. Every demon knows their rank, position and job description. In the kingdom of God it is very important to understand God's Divine Order. Satan does not defeat believers because they are weak; he sometimes defeats them because they do not understand or respect divine order.

> *"And He gave some, apostles; and some, prophets; and some, evangelists; and some pastors and teachers; For the perfecting of the saints, for the work of the ministry, for the edifying of the body of Christ:"*
> *(Ephesians 4:11-12)*

As outlined in *Ephesians 4:11-12, the order of the Church is first the apostles, then the prophets, then the evangelists, then the pastors and then the teachers.* This five-fold ministry team works together in order to demonstrate the kingdom of God in the earth.

> *"And these signs shall follow them that believe; In my name shall they cast out devils; they shall speak with new tongues; They shall take up serpents; and if they drink any deadly thing, it shall not hurt them; they shall lay hands on the sick, and they shall recover."*
> *(Mark 16:17-18)*

The Apostle is called, chosen and sent out by God. As the Greek word *Apostolos* suggests, God commissions this person to build, pioneer and advance His kingdom. This office represents governmental structure and establishes

God's divine order in the kingdom. Apostles are concerned with the global functions in the Body of Christ. He is looked upon as chief in command and is an Overseer who moves in great faith and power.

The Apostle can function in almost every area in ministry. One such example is the Apostle Paul who we saw operated as a preacher, teacher, evangelist, deliverer, counselor, psalmist and more. He is not only concerned about his local church but has a burden and global vision for his neighborhood, city, and the kingdom at large. Further, Apostles seek to raise up new churches, laying firm foundations of structure and order. *(1 Corinthians 3:10)*

He should be blameless, whether married or not and be willing to be a spiritual father to those he leads. Jesus was the Chief Apostle *(Hebrews 3:1)* and when He was ready to commission His disciples, He also sent them out as *Apostles.* *(Matthew 10:1–4)*

The Prophet represents the voice of God to the people. The prophet gives direction, correction, comfort, and edification. The prophet gives accurate, audible messages from God to the people. Prophecy, therefore, can be related to past, present or future events.

Prophets must be called and chosen by God and have legal spiritual authority to operate in the office of the prophet. Otherwise, one can have the gift of prophecy, or operate in the spirit of prophecy.

The person operating *in the office of the prophet* lives in this office. They are called and mandated by God to this office as we saw Elijah, Elisha, Samuel, Huldah, Isaiah, Jeremiah and so many others. For the most part, the office of the prophet can be lonely and in some cases, misunderstood. They speak only what "thus saith the Lord" without compromise; accurately declaring God's Word. They may be used to give clear direction, prediction, edification, comfort, or even rebuke and correction.

The gift of prophecy is a gift, which allows a person to discern and speak forth things into your life as the Spirit gives utterance.

The *spirit or grace of prophecy* can rest upon an individual allowing them to bring forth a message from God, which eventually lifts from them when they are finished with the prophetic "assignment." Further, prophecy reveals the will, purpose, and plan of God in your life." The new dimensional shift of the prophetic will be the prophets who create miracles by the words of their mouth. *(See more in book by author, The Power Of Prophetic Reversal.)*

"... the testimony of Jesus is the spirit of prophecy." (Revelation 19:10)

The Evangelist has been anointed by God to spread the gospel with the purpose of bringing souls into the kingdom. The evangelist loves outreach and will do whatever it takes to advance the kingdom of God most times outside the walls of the local church. Jesus walked in every office, especially that of an evangelist, and so should you.

The Pastor takes care of the flock of God. The Greek word for Pastor, *poimen (pronounced poy-mane)* denotes leading, guiding, and nurturing. He must ensure at all times that this is being done. Pastors should never abuse, use, intimidate or manipulate their flock. Each sheep is different and the wisdom of God will be needed to know how to deal with each one.

The Teacher has been anointed by God to instruct, educate and inform the Body of Christ. The teacher anointing trains the believer to know God through Biblical principles and sound doctrine. They are very administrative and can be used in the local church to keep records, even as the scribes did in the Bible. The Teacher's Anointing is very important and should be overseen by an Apostle, to offer guidance.

CULTIVATING THE FRUIT OF THE SPIRIT
"But the fruit of the spirit is Love, Joy, Peace, Longsuffering, Gentleness, Goodness, Faith, Meekness, Temperance ..."
(Galatians 5:22-23)

There are many prophetic gifting in the Body of Christ. These are special God-inspired abilities which are designed to edify the believer. However, it is very important that those who carry these special ministry gifts also spend time cultivating the fruit of the spirit in their lives.

In *1 Corinthians 13*, the Apostle Paul warns that it can be spiritually detrimental and profit you nothing to operate in a spiritual gift but not have the love of God which is the fruit of the spirit.

Just like every tree needs water, sunlight, soil and the right atmospheric conditions to grow, so do you as a believer need the fruit of the Spirit cultivated in your life.

Spending time daily in worship, prayer, fasting and studying the Word of God are basic components to massive cultivation of the fruit of the Spirit.

Once the fruit has grown to a place of spiritual maturity it becomes ripe and is ready to reproduce after its own kind and ready to flow in harmony with the gifts of the Spirit.

*"...neither shall your vine cast her fruit before the
time in the field, saith the Lord of hosts"
(Malachi 3:11)*

Good Fruit Makes Good Salad

I strongly advise, however, that before you go after the *gifts* of the Spirit you should earnestly seek to cultivate the *fruit* of the Spirit in your life. *(Galatians 5:22-23)*

Many believers make the horrible mistake of running from conference to conference; from church to church in search of a quick impartation. They are eager to prophesy, lay hands on the sick, and in some cases even cast out demons without harnessing the fruit of the Spirit.

Simon the Sorcerer in *Acts 8*, even after his conversion by Philip, sought to extort the gifts from Peter. Peter rebuked him and cast the unclean spirit out of him. Many Christians are like Simon today.

They desire to have the power but are not willing to pay the "spiritual" price, which requires spending time in the presence of God. This is a spiritual indictment against the kingdom and each believer should strive for inner holiness rather than sensationalism.

*"But seek ye first the kingdom of God and his
righteousness and all these things shall be
added unto you." (Matthew 6:33)*

CHAPTER TWELVE

PROPHETIC WARRIOR ANOINTINGS

THE NEHEMIAH (NEHEMIACH) ANOINTING

A prophetic watchman intercedes and builds walls of protection. These "walls" can be built around your home, family, anointing, ministry and life and must be fortified and maintained through prayer.

Nehemiah, as you know, was a cupbearer to the King but he never forgot his kingly assignment to God. He maintained a burden for Jerusalem and was extremely concerned to see how the city and the wall laid waste. He petitioned the King to do the work and was able to find the right people with the same burden to help him. He refused to come down from building, even in the face of adversity.

If you are going to be a powerful prophetic watchman and an Intercessor, you must:
- have a burden about something
- be broken before God
- be willing to petition the King for the anointing to do the task
- be able to gather the right people to work with you
- be willing to fight to the finish

Beware of three (3) evil spirits which seek to distract or to attack believers who walk in the Nehemiach Anointing *(Nehemiah 6:1–4).*

These diabolical spirits are:
- Sanbalot – distraction
- Tobiah – deception
- Gershem – death

Nehemiah never left the wall. He simply said, *"I am doing a great work and will not come down."* Even while working in our everyday lives we cannot forget the specific mandates God gave us.

As Nehamiah rebuilt the walls around the city of Jerusalem to fortify and protect it, so must the walls first be rebuilt in our lives through prayer and supplication. As we find ourselves becoming strengthened, we can begin to stand on the "rebuilt walls of the city" of our lives, as keen, alert and vigilant prophetic watchmen.

THE ESTHER (ESTHERIC) PROPHETIC WARRIOR ANOINTING

Esther was called to the kingdom just in time. Wicked conspirators were planning to destroy the Jews. She had to be reminded of her purpose as a warrior and she immediately called a solemn fast and later a feast.

As warriors you must remember that regardless of where we live, work or go to church, God has a purpose for you being there. Esther and all the Jews fasted and prayed for three (3) days, then prepared a feast to gain victory over her enemies.

You must incorporate fasting in your mission. Every warrior throughout the entire Bible fasted before God to gain the victory in their battles, you must do the same.

Esther had twelve months of preparation. Twelve represents governmental order. She did not know that she would have come up against a Machiavellian ruling spirit in Haman. This season of preparation prepared her for it.

For the Jews, not only was she able to gain the victory but her enemy Haman died on the very gallows he had prepared for Mordecai. Whenever we fast, pray, and obey the voice of God, He defeats our enemies right before our eyes.

To walk in the Estheric Warrior Anointing, you must:
- repare yourself for months, or years , in some cases
- soak in oils and sweet fragrance - the oil represents the anointing and the sweet fragrances represent the presence of God.
- be willing to please the King
- be willing to fast and pray *(See Chapter 5 on Sacrifice)*
- be willing to risk your own life and perish – in other words if it means your life as a warrior you must be willing to die for the cause of the kingdom.

THE JOSEPH (JOSEPHIC) PROPHETIC WARRIOR ANOINTING

Joseph walked in a powerful apostolic, prophetic anointing that impacted fields, cities, and entire regions. This anointing was both apostolic and prophetic in nature, in that it released prosperity and increase, affecting scores of lives, including his family. He was more concerned about the deliverance of his family rather than their destruction.

The colors in his coat represented diversities of the anointings upon his life, even as it relates to the ability to impact a variety of ethnicities and nationalities. The anointing that God had placed upon him translated him from a pitiful situation to a palatial palace. *Seek to walk in the Josephic Anointing today!*

THE EZRA (EZRIACH) PROPHETIC WARRIOR ANOINTING

Ezra, a prophet of God, throughout the entire book of Ezra, compelled Israel to return and rebuild their spiritual relationship with God the Father and restored worship back by reconstructing the altar of God.

Unlike Nehemiah, Ezra was more concerned about rebuilding Israel's spiritual awareness back to God. The children of Israel had experienced so many seasons of bondage in their lives that their Babylonian captivity had somewhat erased their awareness of God.

There must be prophetic watchers and intercessors who are praying that an awareness of and reverence for God remain in their nation, cities, homes and the people around them. As a believer you should always be careful not to mix the holy things of God with that which is profane.

"Light has no fellowship with darkness."

In *Ezra 4:2-5* when their adversaries came to Zerubbabel to help them build the temple, he immediately rejected their offer to help even though they claimed to worship the same God. Zerubbabel was able to discern their diabolical plans and denied their offer to help build God's temple. When you are called by God to do a specific assignment, the enemy may try to pretend to be on your side in order to bring total destruction to your vision.

Bishlam, Mithredath, and Tabeel *(Ezra 4:7)* were the names of three of the evil conspirators who were sent out to conspire against the people of God. They were descendents of Esarhaddon of Assyria who intermarried with the Israelites, which had adopted pagan religions and were then called Samaritans. The true Jews wanted to have nothing to do with them. *(2 Kings 17:24-33; John 4:9)*

Be careful of these ancient spirits of deception and confusion: Bishlam, Mithredath, and Tabeel. They all answer to an Assyrian principality named Esarhaddon.

These spirits normally conspire with the spirit of Jezebel to destroy the apostolic and prophetic churches. In Jude verse 4, it speaks of certain men who crept in unawares.

The increasing presence of the New Age Movement and Human Secularism seem to be advancing through corridors subverting the innocent and deceiving the ignorant even within the walls of the church. God is depending on those of you with the Ezra anointing to pray like never before that righteousness, holiness, and truth will prevail eternally.

THE JOSIAH (JOSIACH) KINGLY ANOINTING

Josiah, the King was also called by God with a powerful anointing. *(2 Kings 22:1)* At the age of eight (8) he was elevated to the throne as King over Judah. Most of his predecessors had served idols and forgotten the Word of God. Josiah made the people search the rubbles of the Temple that had been broken down. It was amongst these rubbles where they found the laws and the Holy Scriptures.

Immediately, Josiah had all the altars of Baal and the houses of the Sodomites destroyed, along with their prophets. Further, he brought spiritual life back to the people of God, reformed the laws and made a covenant with God. In this hour, God is raising up prophetic warriors of all ages with kingly assignments. The prophet Jeremiah walked in a powerful warrior anointing at a very young age. This anointing was, *"...to root out, and to pull down, and to destroy, and throw down, to build, and to plant." (Jeremiah 1:10)*

Even though Josiah was only eight years old, he carried out his divine mandate. During his rule, Josiah accomplished many things for God.

If you are going to walk in a Josiach warrior anointing, you must be willing to:
- dig through the rubbles; although situations may appear to be broken up, God is somewhere in it
- break down the false altars of Baal and Sodomites; break down false religions and ideologies even if they came through generational or ancestral ties
- restore the law and cut covenant with God. God is a God of covenant. He made promises to Abraham that are, to this day, in effect. A covenant is a binding agreement between you and God through the blood of Jesus to serve Him eternally

- build back the altar of God – calling people back to seeking God
- restore spiritual awareness – bring the people back to the knowledge of God and how to serve Him by rebuilding the altars of prayer, praise, and worship.

THE SAMUEL (SAMUELIC) PROPHETIC WARRIOR ANOINTING

Most people recognize Samuel as one of the greatest prophets in Israel. From childhood, he was given to God by his mother, Hannah. He had been brought into the temple at a time where there was no open vision, the Word of God was precious and the lamp of God had gone out where the Ark of God was.

Eli who was the existing priest of that day, his eyes had gone dim and his sons were evil in the sight of God. *(1 Samuel 3:1-3)*

Samuel grew and ministered before the Lord as a child and was able to bring spiritual revival back to Israel, leading them into repentance and by returning the Ark of God to its rightful place. *(1 Samuel 7:3-6)* Not only was he a prophet, but he was also a judge.

The Samuelic Anointing upon your life will:
- bring dedication to God
- create open visions
- bring divine order to your life and the life of others
- cause you to raise up and "anoint" kings and priests
- help to bring to light the revelation and the testimony of Jesus to reality in the lives of others

The great anointings that these men and women walked in are not limited to gender or age but can manifest in the life of any individual who makes himself available to the call of God.

THE CHILDREN'S BREAD

Many of the prophetic warrior anointings were released on young people. Josiah was eight years old when he began to rule; King David was only a teenager when Samuel first anointed him; Joseph was only a child when he began having dreams that he would be great one day. It seems as though God seeks to anoint young people to bring radical change to the overall social, economic, moral and spiritual climates within a region.

For this reason, it seems as though this generation of young people, has been under brutal satanic attacks. Referred to by the world as "Generation X", satan, through sexual promiscuity, negative music, drugs, and violence, has sought to destroy what I call "Generation Excellent."

In fact, from the very beginning satan employed Pharaoh to kill every newborn male child in Egypt, however, it was the hand of God that preserved Moses. Similarly, Herod attempted to kill Jesus by issuing the same decree, however, the hand of God once again intervened and Jesus' life was preserved.

In both accounts, the enemy's attempt to destroy the Deliverer – the one God had ordained to deliver His people in that generation – was unsuccessful. Although these weapons were formed, they did not prosper. On the other hand, the lives of many other infants were sinisterly destroyed.

I believe that just as satan tried to destroy their lives, he is now trying to destroy the lives of this chosen generation.

Even as God is able to anoint and use children, so is satan able to operate through or totally possess them. Lucifer is no respect of people. If a teenager or child willfully opens a door inviting satan to come into his life. Satan, being the thief, destroyer and the deceiver that he is, will come in. (*See the account in Matthew 15*)

David writes in *Psalm 24:6, "This is the generation of them that seek him, that seek thy face, O Jacob..."* I believe, as never before, that it is time to fight for the preservation of this generation. Satan is using subtle, lethal weapons of mass destruction through ancient demons, to try to slow them down and, eventually, wipe them out.

A GENERATION UNDER SIEGE

Teenage pregnancy, drugs (marijuana and cocaine), rock music, are the "old problems", but he has now blended a mixture of homosexuality and lesbianism right into it all, perverting their minds and convincing teenagers that there is nothing wrong with these acts.

In other words, he seeks to persuade them that it is "okay" to be "gay" and that God made a mistake when he created them. The message is subtle and subliminal, if you do not want to be what God has created you, you have the power of choice and can become whatever you want to be; for example, a transvestite, drag queen, cross dresser, etc.

Once again, this is all a part of Satan's diabolical plans to sabotage the lives of our youth and teenagers. Many teenagers or children may also suffer from other social ills such as:

Negative Peer Pressure	*Gang Affiliations*
Low Self-Esteem	*Anxiety*
Gang Violence	*Depression*

Fear of Rejection	*Insecurity*
A Lack Of Identity	*Deception*
Materialism	*Isolation*
Rebellion	*Being Withdrawn*
Anger/Rage	*Child Labor*
Lying	*Divorce* (by way of Parents' divorce)

It is amazing that some of the Asian countries make these violent, satanic video games but do not allow their kids to play them. However, we in the Western world allow our kids access to them, who eventually become addicted and overtaken by spirits of violence and aggression.

Our school corridors are darkened by these lewd, blatant behaviors. Mutual female relationships that we once called "girlfriends" are now *"GIRLFRIENDS"*. These once platonic relationships have now been perverted into erroneous, intimate ones.

To further the confusion, some girls are presenting themselves as masculine while some boys are displaying feminine mannerisms, as our society embraces it as the "norm". It is important to note that "teenagers will be teenagers". We should not make the mistake of judging a young lady that is athletic as masculine, or a boy who loves to cook, as feminine.

However, it is vitally important that we teach our young people to appreciate exactly who they are in God. It is important that we teach them to understand that, with whatever gender they were born, that is what God has created and intended them to be. Encouraging them, from early childhood, to celebrate their innate identity will prevent them from suffering a major identity crisis later in life.

144

Some children are now seeking to rule parents and so many parents, struggle trying to establish or re-establish their moral values. It is sad, however, that others have been swept away and have accepted such abominable behaviors.

RECLAIMING A GENERATION

We cannot idly sit by and watch the enemy destroy our young people. We must begin to pray against this lewd, erotic spirit that has been released to subvert the minds of our children and teenagers. We must pray against the negative effects of the media and Hollywood that are partly responsible for the overt and indecent exposure of pornographic material and movies. This exploitation is adding further confusion to the minds of our young people.

We must go back to the basics and teach our children the dangers of some secular music and how it negatively impacts their lives. This is all-important for the preservation of this generation.

For the past several years, my husband and I have had youth and family rallies, marches, concerts, revivals, seminars and radio segments dealing with the moral state of our youth. Although we were supported by thousands of young people, we were amazed as to how many pastors, political leaders and adults took issue with what we were doing.

We were ridiculed as we took a righteous stand against vexing ills which were destroying our young people. The reason for their lack of support was because they said that *"youth issues"* had always been around and will never be resolved, so we should just leave them alone.

Chainbreaking Results

After a huge rally in 2005 and live radio talk show, the phone at my office never stopped ringing. People were calling from everywhere. People were pleading and begging for help, either for themselves or relatives who were struggling with personal issues.

This convinced me that not everyone involved in "alternative lifestyles" wanted to be involved in them. In fact, during our deliverance breakthrough revivals for youth, we discovered that many of them were victims of incest, rape, molestation or were simply lured into this lifestyle by demonized adults who themselves had been victims of the same things.

"Fighting for the preservation of our youth involves spiritual warfare."

We must earnestly contend for their survival. We must pray to stop the violence amongst teens. We must snatch them out of the claws of "greedy" drug dealers and hungry pimps who only want to exploit their bodies.

We must discourage our youth from satanic chat rooms and addictive, erotic websites and begin to show them that Jesus is Lord and Master of the Universe, and that He has called them with a divine purpose and destiny.

This is the generation, as I foresaid, that will usher in the greatest move of God. This generation will prophesy and do more than any other generation has done. Thus, let each of us take the time to teach them the principles of the kingdom of God, including worship and, definitely, spiritual warfare.

As a parent, you must be willing to give your child(ren) to God for His use; the hand of *God is always on the children.* One of the things that concern me is that the world's system has no problem in using and pushing their children.

In fact, you do not need to look far to see our television and radio broadcasts filled with young and upcoming secular artists. Kids, for the most part, are being exploited and used as sex objects and sold as slaves to the highest bidders.

The world's greed for money and power has placed leashes around the necks of our children and have forced them to fall prey to some of the most horrific situations imaginable such as: drug use and abuse, pornography, prostitution, child molestation, rape and other forms of exploitation.

For the most part, many churches waste time babysitting their children instead of training them to become spiritual warriors. Parents, on the other hand, allow the television to nurture their kids because they are too busy to do so. Because of a lack of parental involvement, children are daily being exposed to pornography on the internet, playing with subliminal forms of witchcraft such as tarot cards, ouija boards, Harry Potter fantasy books, and their horoscope.

This generation has been used, abused and over-exposed to so many elements of the demonic kingdom of darkness, that by the time they go to church on Sunday, there is little or no interest in the things of God.

There are many parents going to church Bible studies, leaving their children home under the misconception that they will not understand the preacher anyway. These are all satanic leashes and are all intended to ensnare and bind up this generation.

Over the past years, while traveling to preach the gospel, I was always concerned about the youth and children. I believe that this is the great army that Joel saw in *Joel 2:7*:

> *"They shall run like mighty men; they shall*
> *climb the wall like men of war; and they shall*
> *march every one on his ways, and they shall*
> *not break their ranks:"*

REVIVAL IS COMING

And finally, I believe that God will pour His spirit upon this generation and they shall prophesy, dream dreams, see visions, and usher in one of the greatest revivals the world has ever seen. *(Joel 2:28)*

Your children should be trained first of all to know and love God. The Bible declares that we ought to:

> *"Train up a child in the way he should go: and*
> *when he is old, he will not depart from it"*
> *(Proverbs 22:6)*

Therefore, we must all begin to engage in spiritual warfare, intercepting the plans which the enemy has for our children. God has commanded us to take hold of the rungs of the altar to bring substantial changes in their lives.

Waiting until our children are completely rebellious, standing before a criminal court judge, in a drug unit or worst of all, dead, is not the time for us to begin praying.

*"... the kingdom of heaven suffereth violence,
and the violent take it by force."
(Matthew 11:12)*

We must begin to aggressively bind up the spirits of rebellion, violence, perversion, lust, materialism, *"remedialcy"* and release the spirit of obedience, gratitude, discipline, chastity, abstinence, security, peace, unity, knowledge, a quick understanding, love and the spirit of life to operate in and through their lives. Finally, your children should be trained how to worship God and do spiritual warfare. This generation is not lost – they have simply been misguided. They are curious to learn the ways of the kingdom.

I declare that all false altars are broken down and burned by the fire of God, in Jesus' name. I believe that the gifts of miracles, signs, and wonders will manifest in phenomenal ways, even through the lives of youth and children. *(1 Corinthians 12:7–11)*

PRAYER FOR OUR CHILDREN

Father God, I worship and exalt You. I reverence you for who you are and what you mean to me. I worship you because you are mighty and sovereign, because you are God and beside you there is no other.

I bring our children and the youth of our nation before you and all things concerning them. I pull down and break all generational and ancient curses from over the lives of our children, I bind up every spirit of rebellion that would cause our children to be rebellious against their parents and elders, every spirit that would seek to cause them to engage in premarital sex, unnatural sexual acts, lewd lust and any other associated spirits and we bind up the strongholds of perversion from over their lives.

We take authority over every unclean spirit of addiction such as drugs, marijuana, alcohol, cocaine, ecstasy, sex, food and every other drug they may seek to use, and we bind up the stronghold of addiction. We release a hunger for God and the things that are of God. We take control over the spirits of lying, deception, and stealing and we replace them with the spirits of honesty and truth.

Every spirit of pain, hurt, disappointment, rejection, hatred, every mind battling spirit: loose your stronghold from off of the minds of the children. Get out, and go to the bottom of the ocean; and I decree that the judgment of the Lord Jesus be upon you. I declare that every spirit of Learning Disability (LD) and Mental Disorders – Attention Deficit (Hyperactivity) Disorders (ADHD); Behavioral Emotional Handicap Disorders (BEHD); Mental Retardation Disorder (MRD); and every other disorder which may cause them not to retain what is being taught; every spirit of autism, every slow and remedial spirit: we command you to go from out of our children's lives. We release the Holy Spirit to be at work in them that they would possess the spirit of wisdom and understanding that will cause them to excel in school.

Every spirit of peer-pressure, low self-esteem, insecurity and gang affiliation that would seek to make them think less of who they are and compromise their principles and values that have been instilled in them, every spirit that would make them want to fit in, we bind, loose and break it from over their lives, in Jesus' name.

We bind, loose, and break every spirit of sabotage that may seek to discourage and frustrate our children to abort the call of God on their lives. We release you from your assignment and summons you to go right now from their lives in the name of Jesus. We sever every ungodly soul tie in their lives to things, ungodly friendships, or relationships that may cause them to lose focus of their calling, and we ask that you do a work in their hearts, their minds and their spirits. And we speak life into them that they would be young men and young women set apart unto you.

Now Father we take authority over these spirits and release the fruit and gifts of the Spirit (Galatians 5:22-23 and 1 Corinthians 12:4-10) to operate in their lives.

Now Father God, we take authority over every unclean spirit and ungodly influences and we release your warring angels that excel in strength and power to war on our behalf to fight with flaming swords of fire and intercept all plots or plans for our children's lives so that they may come into the full understanding of who You are.

We seal this prayer right now under the blood of Jesus.
Amen!!

CHAPTER THIRTEEN

～◇◇◇◇◇～

GOD'S SOLDIERS ON THE BATTLEFIELD

DRESSED FOR BATTLE

God is very concerned about soldiers in His army. When you sign up for "the service", it is one thing to be in the army and another thing to be in war. You must be dressed for battle and ready to fight. You must have at least gone through spiritual boot camp and have an idea as to who your real enemy is.

When you come into the army of God, the very day that you confess Jesus as Lord you were enlisted for warfare. It is no more by choice or by chance but, you automatically, engages in battle.

You life is no longer your own. But just as someone enlists in their country's army, you are now enlisted in the army of the Kingdom of God. *(1Corinthians 6:20)* You must now dress yourself with spiritual garments or prayer, praise and worship as you prepare for warfare.

AS LONG AS YOU ARE ON THE BATTLEFIELD, YOU MUST WORSHIP BECAUSE THERE WILL BE WARFARE.

CASUALTIES IN SPIRITUAL WARFARE

Over the years, there have been so many "senseless" casualties. The Church was accustomed to and was taught all about *Worship*, but hardly anyone taught about *Spiritual Warfare*.

On the other hand, most believers have mastered the art of spiritual defense, but have very little or no knowledge at all about spiritual offense. In other words, we know how to cry out and pray the "Lord, I need you" prayers, but have not learnt how to effectively command, siege, pursue and take back what the enemy has stolen from us.

Spiritual Defense is to block what is being shot at you but *Spiritual Offense* is to get up and fire at the enemy, taking what is rightfully yours.

The Word of God clearly states in Jude verse 3 *"that we should earnestly contend for the faith that was once delivered unto us."* The word *"contend"* means to fight, engage in battle. The word "earnestly", in this case, means not giving up until you have fully secured the goods. In other words, salvation is free, but you have got to pay a daily sacrificial price in warfare to maintain it.

HARD BALLS

Life will throw many hard balls at you as a Soldier. Missiles will come from all directions but you must know how to fight and recover all from these life-threatening blows. It is always easier to give up. In fact, the first human notion

154

when faced with crisis is to give up. Satan tries to convince you that you do not really need to fight, just give up and die.

I have had many of these moments in my life when life threw hard balls at me. There were times that I was hit so hard that the only thing I wanted to do was bury my head in the sand. I know about crying all night long, feeling hurt, rejected, suicidal, but the next morning the problem was still there. It was not until I made a decision that enough was enough, that I was no longer running from the devil and his demons, but had them running from me.

DO NOT BREAK RANK!

To "not break rank" means to *not* compromise your spiritual position under any circumstances but rather God is calling on you to submit yourself to godly spiritual leadership and allow the gift from the Spirit of God to be cultivated in you. There is no time to make a pact or negotiate with the devil. God is looking for real soldiers in the army, real warriors. You must remain resolute and faithful to the finish. Do not bow down, do not break your rank or leave the army!

In *Joel 2:7*, God speaks of a powerful young army he is raising up; one that shall run up walls and climb through windows, seizing what belongs to them and not giving up.

Shadrach, Meshach and Abednego were resolute in their faith. They made it known to Nebuchadnezzar that they were not bowing down to any image. It is very important that you do not bow down to any image even the ones that come to your mind. As a soldier, one of your assignments is to cast down imaginations or any high thing that exalteth itself against who Christ is in you. *(2 Corinthians 10:5)*

155

It is vitally important that God's soldiers always remember that the spiritual battleground can be anywhere: in the ghetto, prostitute houses, on your job, in school, in government offices, or anywhere satan chooses to set up demon spirits to hinder you.

We are fighting in a real war that is waged in the realm of the spirit. Therefore, the person next to you is not your enemy. Your enemy is the devil and he is on the opposite side of the battlefield. Ephesians 6:12 says, *"For we wrestle not against flesh and blood."* Most people waste their time fighting each other.

For example, wives waste time arguing with their unsaved husbands, calling them the "devil"; church members engage in contentious struggles with each other and in some cases, the pastor; employees become frustrated with overbearing supervisors, bosses; and even parents may become discouraged over disobedient and rebellious children.

Mark 11:23 says, *you shall have whatsoever you say.* It is so important that we begin to address the real culprit, so that you will understand that these people are not your enemies and they are not who you are fighting against. The real culprit is the devil himself – satan, the deceiver of the world, Lucifer, accuser of the brethren, beelzebub the father of lies, he is your enemy. Call the demon spirit that is seeking to destroy your money, marriage or family by his name. Bind him up and cast him out in Jesus' name!

As God's soldier, you have already been given delegated authority to cast out devils in Jesus' name. *(See more in Chapter on Breaking The Chains.)* Be bold, be strong and *"... let the weak say, I am strong,"* God will fight for you. *(Joel 3:10)*

STAY YOUR POSITION

After you have done everything to stand, stand fast. You cannot afford to give up in the midst of your fight.   As the Word of God says in *1 Corinthians 15:58*, you must be steadfast, unmovable, always abounding in the work of the Lord, for your labour shall not be in vain.   Christian soldiers who understand the importance of being in this Spiritual Army will never retreat to the enemy's camp.

The Bible says in *2 Timothy 2:20* that *"in a great house, there are not only vessels of gold, and of silver, but also of wood and of earth..."*. Regardless of what the vessels are made of, they are all important. In *1 Corinthians 12:14* there are many members but one body.

If the whole body were an eye, how would we hear? And if the whole body were an ear, how will we see? God made each Christian soldier with unique abilities and features. You must begin to tap into the things of God and find out exactly what your area of expertise is. In the meantime, keep on worshipping. *Your worship will bring revelation.*

MARCHING SOLDIERS

Marching plays an integral role in the life of a soldier and warrior. In fact, one of the first routines established during any boot camp is that of training the battalion to march.   The march is synchronized and orchestrated to display unity and strength. It denotes discipline and structure. Each step is calculated and in stride with the previous one.

I have always been fascinated by the way soldiers would march but never fully understood their purpose for doing so until several years ago. We started an early Morning

Prayer service at our local church. Scores of people would rush through the doors at 5:30 a.m. each morning, but within ten minutes of their arrival, they would all be fast asleep on the altar.

I was very frustrated and became angry, because not only were these people under attack in their personal lives, but also the church itself was going through tremendous persecution. The Holy Spirit spoke to me and told me to put on some soft worship music and tell the people to begin to march up and down as they prayed.

For the first several weeks this seemed difficult for many people, but after a few months, people began testifying about the supernatural breakthroughs they were having in their prayer lives that eventually overflowed in every area of their personal lives.

Almost seven years later we are still having the 5:30 a.m. prayer every morning and adults, even children, are still marching up and down praying. The marching not only made them physically energized but it also kept them spiritually alert. This corporate marching to and fro on one accord helps to develop strength and spiritual stamina, something we could not ordinarily do by ourselves. God, through the spirit of unity, has brought total deliverance and glorious victory to us.

The Bible clearly states that satan is under our feet. In fact, in *Genesis 3:15* it says, **the seed of the woman shall bruise his (satan's) head.** Furthermore, if we are still seated with Christ in heavenly places, then that puts satan's demonic powers beneath us. Much too often Christians make the mistake of allowing satan to feel all powerful by pointing upwards to him when he is really under our feet as a defeated foe in Jesus' name.

By marching to and fro as a soldier while worshipping and praying, you are literally claiming territories and regions. God told Abraham that every place the sole of his feet went was his and his seed's, throughout all his generations. God has promised the earth to man, in fact, we have the legal authority here; it is our domain.

THE POWER OF MARCHING

In *2 Kings 7* the Bible accounts a story about four lepers that were cast outside their city and left to die. They, no doubt, like many religious folks had begun to discuss all the things they had tried whilst in pursuit of their deliverance from death and disease. The Bible says they were sitting outside of the gate waiting to die.

They had tried praying, shouting, scratching, creeping, even begging, so as not to go to sleep. Finally, they decided to do something different. It was illegal and not to mention, unorthodox. They knew that it was time to take their worship to the next level. *It was time to warfare!*

The four lepers began marching to and fro. At first they were frail, faint and tired. They were hungry, sick and broke. Their death sentence was pending but they boldly did what no other lepers had ever done before. The Bible states that as they began to march towards the enemy's camp, God made their feet sound like an entire army. The Syrians who were archenemies of Israel became very afraid and all fled for their lives, leaving behind their tents loaded with food, money, clothing and precious stones. The four lepers could not believe what they saw. They ate to their heart's content and brought their entire nation out of poverty into prosperity and victory.

Marching to and fro is very important in the life of a soldier and warrior. It helps us to regain territories and access into new dimensions.

Satan walks to and fro in the earth, claiming territories. Therefore, we, as true heirs of the promise should also, at times, walk up and down during prayer to reclaim territories in the realm of the spirit? Marching soldiers return home after the battle is over and wave their banners of victory. Strive to become a marching soldier today and walk your way into your victory.

"He maketh my feet like hinds' feet..."
(Psalm 18:33)

"For by thee I have run through a troop, and
by my God have I leaped over a wall."
(Psalm 18: 29)

As we saw earlier, a spiritual Intercessor is one who builds walls of protection through prayer. However in the context of Psalm 18:29, the troops and walls mentioned here are spiritual legions of demons which have been set up to create barriers, hindrances, and obstacles. By marching to and fro you become spiritually militant, defeating principalities and eradicating their powers, coming out with the imminent victory.

In Joshua 6 God had promised Joshua that He would give them the victory over Jericho. Not many armies had defeated Jericho, mainly because of its high walls and towers. The wall was so huge that almost six chariots could ride on the top of it side by side. The only strategy God gave Joshua was to worship, march around the wall for seven days and on the seventh day - seven times - and shout. The Bible said when they did this Jericho's walls came tumbling down. This form of worship and warfare gave Israel a glorious victory and Jericho was totally destroyed.

Jesus told His disciples to watch and pray. Religion makes you feel that unless you close your eyes while worshipping or praying, God will not hear you. But I believe when you are engaged in hostile combat that you will need to keep your eyes wide open. This watchfulness keeps you sharp and alert so that you can precisely hit your target, the enemy.

> *"For we walk by faith and not by sight."*
> *(2 Corinthians 5:7)*

ENDURING HARDNESS

Paul told Timothy to endure hardness as a good soldier and to fight the good fight of faith. The champion in a boxing match is not always the one with all the muscles and mouth. Normally it is the boxer who, despite his painful blows, cuts and bruises, is able to remain standing even in the final round after the tenth count.

God is looking for His soldiers that have tenacity, endurance and the ability to stick and stay after all the hard blows dealt by life, have been hurled at them.

When the sons of God came before God in *Job 1:6-7*, satan also showed up from walking to and fro in the earth. God asked him if he had heard about his servant Job. Obviously satan did because he was able to tell God that Job only served Him because of the hedge of protection around him. God gave satan the permission to go to battle against Job but satan was not allowed to take his life. God already knew the heart of Job and that he would endure this test.

CHAPTER FOURTEEN

THE FIGHT FOR YOUR SOUL

PREPARE FOR WAR

We must remember that we are engaged in a relentless war that is taking place in the realm of the spirit. This spiritual war is being fought between the kingdom of darkness, led by Lucifer, himself, and the kingdom of light, led by Jehovah, the King of kings and the Lord of lords, and is for the ultimate possession of your soul.

Both kingdoms function similarly to how we see some earthly kingdoms operate; under established laws, seeking to protect and fortify itself, advancing its interests while gaining new territories.

These spiritual kingdoms have already been established in the realm of the spirit and they are now seeking to become established in the earth realm. When Jesus taught His disciples to pray, in Matthew 6:10, He teaches them to ask the Father to let His kingdom be established in earth even as it is in heaven.

> *"Thy kingdom come. Thy will be done on
> earth, as it is in heaven."*

Also, in the book of Revelations 11:15, it states , *"The kingdoms of this world are become the kingdoms of our Lord, and of His Christ, and He shall reign for ever and ever."*

As Sovereign Ruler, it was always God's intent to rule and reign over His entire universe, including the earth. However, He gave man dominion over the earth realm and sanctioned him as the only agent who should legally operate in this realm. Therefore, if the will of God is to be done in the earth, God must seek out a man that He can use to pour Himself into. Likewise, if satan wants to do anything in the earth realm, he does the same.

Remember, satan's kingdom is the direct antithesis of the kingdom of God. As ambassadors for and servants of the kingdom of God in this earth realm, we should seek to be used by God to promote and advance His commands, interests, will and desires, as we seek to intercept, block or hinder the advancement of satan's demonic kingdom.

THE STRONG MAN
*"...how can one enter into a strong man's
house and spoil his goods, except he first bind
the strong man and then he will spoil his
house." (Matthew 12:29)*

Whenever the enemy gains access into the life of an individual, entity or territory, his first strategy is to set a *"strong man"* in place. The strong man, as its name denotes, seeks to dominate and control your activities. It acts as a doorkeeper by locking, blocking and manipulating the mind, will and emotions and can actually affect your entire life. The strong man seeks to intimidate and manipulate God's divine will and purpose in your life.

For example, God's will is that you prosper and be in health even as your soul prospers. The strong man, called the spirit of INFIRMITY will seek to bring many kinds of sicknesses and diseases upon you.

Strong man spirits will seek to control your life, however, many of them can be "passive aggressive" in nature. The strongman can be explained by considering a basic family structure. If a thief enters a house, he will not bind the baby first. However, he ties up the strongest person, who is usually a man or the strongest family member, then he will strip and rob the house.

Many people struggle in their daily walk with God leading frustrated and confused lives. It is not God's will that any one should perish but that we all come into the knowledge of who God is and what His divine plan and purpose is for us.

Satan knows that each individual's decision to follow Christ will be the best choice he could ever make. His job, therefore, is to ensure that you never totally exercise your authority to bind up the strongman and be set free. He is fully aware of the power of the blood of Jesus. However, he knows that if his strongman is in place, bombarding your life with stress, misery and pain, then serving God could become extremely difficult and even laborious.

IDENTIFYING AND BINDING THE STRONG MAN

In order to live your life to the fullest, you must be willing to identify the strong man that is in your life, bind him, loose him from his assignment and revive the divine will of God in that area of your life.

THERE ARE MANY DEMONIC STRONG MEN WHICH SEEK TO KEEP YOU IN BONDAGE. HERE ARE SOME OF THOSE STRONG MEN AND OTHER SPIRITS WHICH WORK ALONG WITH THEM:

The Spirit of WHOREDOM/HARLOTRY

"My people ask counsel at their stocks, and their staff declareth unto them: for the spirit of whoredoms hath caused them to err, and they have gone a whoring from under their God."
(Hosea 4:12) Also see Hosea 5:4.

Some of the behavioral manifestations can include, but are not limited to:
- Spiritual Idolatry
- Prostitution (Prostitution of the spirit, soul or body)
- Greed
- Lust/Inordinate Desires
- Gluttony (Excessive appetite for anything)
- Spiritual Fornication (Hosea 4:13-19)
- Unfaithfulness/Adultery (Galatians 5:19)

The Spirit of FEAR

"For God hath not given us the spirit of fear; but of power, and of love, and of a sound mind." (2 Timothy 1:7)

Some of the behavioral manifestations can include, but are not limited to:
- Torment/Horror (Irrational Fear)
- Worry/Anxiety/Stress (1 Peter 5:7)
- Phobias
- Nightmares/Night Terrors (Psalm 91:5, 6)
- Heart Attacks (Psalm 55:4)
- Feelings of Inadequacy

166

- Fear of Heights
- Fear of the Dark
- Fear Of Failure
- Fear Of Success
- Fear Of Death

The Spirit of PRIDE (A HAUGHTY Spirit)

"Pride goeth before destruction, and an haughty spirit before a fall." (Proverbs 16:18)

"Better it is to be of an humble spirit with the lowly, than to divide the spoil with the proud." (Proverbs 16:19)

Some of the behavioral manifestations can include, but are not limited to:

- Anger
- Gossip
- Stubbornness
- Wrath
- Arrogance
- Self-righteousness
- "Unteachable"
- Smugness
- Scornfulness
- Strife
- Contentiousness
- Argumentative
- Self-Deception
- Idleness

The Spirit of BONDAGE

"For ye have not received the spirit of bondage again to fear; but ye have received the Spirit of adoption, whereby we cry, Abba, Father" (Roman 8:15)

Some of the behavioral manifestations can include, but are not limited to

- Bitterness
- Addiction (drugs, alcohol, food, etc.)

167

- Unforgiveness
- Manipulation
- Compulsive or Perpetual sin (John 8:34-36)

The Spirit of JEALOUSY

"And his brethren envied him..."
(Genesis 37:11)

Some of the behavioral manifestations can include, but are not limited to:

- Anger/Rage
- Envy
- Covetousness
- Strife/Contention
- Malice
- Hatred
- Competition
- Revenge
- Murder

The Spirit of INFIRMITY

"He sent His Word, and healed them, and delivered them out of their distresses."
(Psalm 107:20)

"But He was wounded for our transgressions, He was bruised for our iniquities: the chastisement of our peace was upon Him; and with His stripes we are healed." (Isaiah 53:5)

Some of the manifested illnesses can include, but are not limited to:

- Cancer
- A.I.D.S.
- Ulcers
- Fibroids
- Heart Disease

- Hypertension
- Blood Disorders (Eg. Anemia, ...)
- Paralysis
- All sicknesses and diseases

A LYING Spirit

20"Then there came out a spirit, and stood before the LORD, and said, I will entice him. And the LORD said unto him, Wherewith?"

21"And he said, I will go out, and be a lying spirit in the mouth of all his prophets. And the Lord said, Thou shalt entice him, and thou shalt also prevail: go out, and do even so."

22"Now therefore, behold, the LORD hath put a lying spirit in the mouth of these thy prophets, and the LORD hath spoken evil against thee."
(2 Chronicles 18:20-22)

Some of the behavioral manifestations can include, but are not limited to:

- False Accusations
- False Teaching
- False Humility
- Gossiping
- Superstition
- Deception
- False Submission
- Insincerity
- Fabrication
- Flattery
- Slander

The Spirit of the ANTI-CHRIST

"Hereby know ye the Spirit of God: Every spirit that confesseth that Jesus Christ is come in the flesh is of God:" 1John 4:2) See also 1 Timothy 4:6.

"And every spirit that confesseth not that Jesus Christ is come in the flesh is not of God: and this is that spirit of antichrist, whereof ye have heard that it should come; and even now already is it in the world." (1 John 4:3)

Some of the behavioral manifestations can include, but are not limited to:
- Denial of Christ
- Denial of the Death, Burial, and Resurrection of Jesus Christ
- Rejection of the Bible
- Heretic Teachings
- Rise of False Doctrines

Spirit of DIVINATION

"And it came to pass, as we went to prayer, a certain damsel possessed with a spirit of divination met us,..." (Acts 16:16a)

"But Paul being grieved, turned and said to the spirit, I command thee in the name of Jesus Christ to come out of her. And he came out the same hour." (Acts 16:18)

Some of the people who practice divination can include, but are not limited to:

- Fortune Tellers/Soothsayers
- Witches/Warlocks/Sorcerers
- Astrologists
- Clairvoyants/Mediums
- Seducers
- Drug Dealers
- Necromancers
- Yoga Practitioners

Some of the behavioral manifestations can include, but are not limited to:

- Drug Abuse
- Water witching
- Occult/Witchcraft Practices
- Rebellion
- Manipulation/Control
- Deception

The Spirit of Divination (FAMILIAR Spirit

"Now the Spirit speaketh expressly, that in the latter times some shall depart from the faith, giving heed to seducing spirits, and doctrines of devils..."
(1 Timothy 4:1; See also 1 Samuel 28:7; Deuteronomy 18:10-12)

Some of the manifestations can include the practice of, but are not limited to:

- Astrology
- Fortune-Telling
- Metaphysical practices
- Transcendental Meditation
- Following your Horoscope

- Occult Practices
- Deception
- Seduction

The Spirit of Seduction

"Now the Spirit speaketh expressly, that in the latter times some shall depart from the faith, giving heed to seducing spirits, and doctrines of devils." *(1 Timothy 4:1)*

Some of the behavioral manifestations can include, but are not limited to:

- Manipulation
- Control
- Disagreement
- Disunity
- Discord/Contention
- Confusion
- Disappointment/Discouragement
- Spiritual Abortion
- Separation
- Notes: Some of these behavioral manifestations can also be demonstrated by someone operating with a familiar spirit.)

The DEAF & DUMB Spirit

"And they bring unto Him one that was deaf, and had an impediment in his speech; and they beseech Him to put His hand upon him." *(Mark 7:32)*

*Some of the behavioral manifestations can
include, but are not limited to:*

- epilepsy
- seizures
- muteness
- stuttering
- suicide
- hearing impediments
- mental illness
- ear problems (ringing in the ear)
- foaming at the mouth

The Spirit of PERVERSION (A PERVERSE Spirit)

*"Flee also youthful lusts: but follow
righteousness, faith, charity, peace, with them
that call on the Lord out of a pure heart."
(2 Timothy 2:22)*

*Some of the behavioral manifestations can
include, but are not limited to:*

- Lust
- Fornication
- Hatred for God *(Proverbs 23:23)*
- Spirit of Error (Doctrinal Error)
- Twisting the Word
- Abortion
- Incest
- Pornography
- Atheism

The Spirit of HEAVINESS

*"To appoint unto them that mourn in Zion, to give unto them
beauty for ashes, the oil of joy for mourning, the garment of
praise for the spirit of heaviness; that they might be called
trees of righteousness, the planting of the LORD, that he
might be glorified." (Isaiah 61:3)*

Some of the behavioral manifestations can include, but are not limited to:

- Grief/Excessive mourning
- Sorrow (Broken Heart)
- Despair
- Hopelessness
- Self-Pity
- A Wounded Spirit

- (Inner Hurts)
- Gloom/Doom
- Rejection
- Depression
- Oppression
- Insomnia
- Disappointment

The Spirits of POVERTY & LACK

"...a little sleep, a little slumber, a little folding of the hands to sleep: So shall thy poverty come as one that travaileth, and thy want as an armed man." (Proverbs 6:10)

"Ye have sown much, and bring in little; ye eat, but ye have not enough; ye drink, but ye are not filled with drink; ye clothe you, but there is none warm; and he that earneth wages earneth wages to put it into a bag with holes." (Haggai 1:6)

Some of the behavioral manifestations can include, but are not limited to:

- Debt
- Deep Sleep/Slumber
- Lack
- Insufficiency
- Limitation
- *(See also Hosea 4:7)*
- *(See also Haggai 1:2-11)*

CHAPTER FIFTEEN

~∞⧉∞~

THE FIGHT FOR YOUR SOUL: POWER OVER UNCLEAN SPIRITS

EXPOSING UNCLEAN/DEMONIC SPIRITS

Unclean/demonic spirits are disembodied spirits, unclean and evil by nature. Further, it is believed by some, that the one-third of angels that fell with Lucifer were cast out of heaven and are now operating under his command. They have names, personalities, mannerisms and characteristics that they portray.

As you know, there are many biblical references to demonic spirits throughout the Bible. Jesus encountered several such spirits that can be classified into 3–4 categories:

- **Unclean spirits** – these spirits *bind* and limit your mobility (ex. fear, doubt and unbelief)
- **Tormenting spirits** – these spirits seek to *attack* your mind, bringing you under their demonic control
- **Evil spirits** – these spirits will totally overtake and possess you, causing you to become heartless as you

perform heinous crimes, violent acts and sexual behaviors. These spirits will also *drive* you to the point where you become compulsive and obsessive in your behavior

- **Seducing spirits** – these spirits will go to any extent to discourage you in an effort to *lure, drag* or *entice* you out of your kingdom assignment and away from the kingdom of God.

- **Familial spirits** - these spirits *travel in the family through your bloodline and* can actively operate in your life by manifesting diseases, hardships, misfortunes and other negative experiences which may drastically limit you. If there are negative "traits" which you can identify that manifest in different members of the same family this is, more than likely, a familial spirit. For example, there may be an ailment or unusual sickness that is common to all members of a family. On the other hand, there may also be a trait of extreme poverty that looms over a family from generation to generation no matter how they seek to break free from it. Many people make the gross mistake of taking ownership of these demonic spirits by making statements such as, "That's just the way I am." "Everybody in my family does this" or "All the men in my family cheat on their wives", not knowing that they are calling unclean or familial spirits to themselves.

- **A Familiar spirit** is a spirit that is assigned to a family and travels from generation to generation attaching itself to a person or people in a family line. It is then sought after for ancient and divine revelations and knowledge; supplying the family with supernatural knowledge, worldly possessions, success, and spiritual wisdom. Further, familiar spirits can act as informants as they observe how the family operates or functions. In turn, this *spirit*, a divining demon, after being conjured up, gives this information to a sorcerer, witch or spirit guide. Spiritism, necromancy, and psychic revelation were believed to come to certain *"gifted"* family members.

However, what many do not realize is that this power or ability was given to them by a demon or *familiar spirit* that satan assigned to their family line. *(Leviticus 20:27; 1 Samuel 28:8)*

SEDUCING SPIRITS:
THE SPIRIT OF SEDUCTION

We must all beware of the spirit of seduction. This is a shrewd and very powerful spirit whose aim and objective is to weary its chosen victim or opponent by sending fiery darts of discouragement and depression to that individual's life.

Its ultimate goal is to cause you to relinquish your position, giving up your power or seat of authority. Remember, the seducer has no need for your power; it is only the officer who has the responsibility of removing you from your kingdom assignment. Your power is turned over to demons called "powers", which activate diabolical laws of hurt, pain, shame, infirmity, etc. in your life. *(see more on "Powers" in Chapter 12)*

These demons are relentless in their fight. They constantly shoot demonic arrows of wickedness at your mind and are the bearers of bad news. They will do everything they can to seek to destroy you. They will even launch a final attack at your "jugular vein" *by using the people nearest to you or trusted friends and loved ones to speak words of doubt and unbelief in your spirit.*

You must stay your position. You must fight to the finish. Be steadfast, unmovable always abounding in the faith. Place your confidence in knowing that God has given you power to command the angels to work on your behalf and these *godly spiritual agents* are now being released to undergird and strengthen you, in Jesus' name.

DELIVERANCE FROM UNCLEAN/DEMONIC SPIRITS

For the most part, unclean/demonic spirits can work alone or in groups or clusters (Mark 5:9). Because God has given us power over them, we can receive total deliverance from them. If you believe that your life is being oppressed by any unclean/demonic spirit, you should seek deliverance through the aid of a prophet or spiritual leader who is anointed to minster deliverance. This deliverance may involve the following:

- calling on the name of Jesus (Romans 10:13; Joel 2:32), casting them out and commanding them to go in Jesus' name (Mark 16:17)
  declaring the Word of God against them (Matthew 4:4,7,10; Matthew 18:18; Isaiah 54:17; Jeremiah 23:29)
  training your hands to do war (Psalm 18:34)
  using a Prayer Cloth or Apron (Acts 19:11-12)
- resisting the devil (James 4:7,8)
- applying the blood of Jesus (Exodus 12:13)
- using Olive Oil (James 5:14)
  using water in different ways (eg. The Pool Of Bethesda–John 5; and Namaan, the Syrian–2 Kings 5)
- Worshipping, Praising and Regularly Giving God Thanks (2 Chronicles 20:1-30; Joshua 6:20)
- praying and fasting (Mark 9:29)

However, it is important to note that you are neither limited to nor restricted by a specific method of deliverance. Jesus knew that evil men and seducers would wax worse and worse. As a result of their strange and ungodly practices they

have released demonic spirits to attach themselves to the lives of many people. Therefore, the task of undoing some of their evil workings may sometimes require unconventional methods.

As a Ministry Leader called to the area of deliverance, please be led by the Spirit of God as you minister deliverance. Your methods, though unconventional, should never go against God's established order or laws. It is important to remember that *Jesus cast out the unclean spirits by the power of His Word.*

The Bible makes many references to unclean spirits. Some of these accounts are found in *Luke 4:33; Mark 1:23-28; Matthew 9:32; and Luke 11:14-26.*

Unclean spirits may be passed down to you through generational curses or you may have opened the doors for them to come in through your own willful sin. The following are some of the more common spirits that I have come in contact with as I have administered deliverance:

- The Spirit of Rebellion
- The Spirit of Pride
- The Spirit of Anger
- The Spirit of Abandonment
- The Spirit of the Occult/Witchcraft
- The Spirit of Addiction
- The Spirit of Fear
- The Spirit of Torment and Pain
- The Spirit of Rejection
- The Spirit of Arrested Development
- The Spirit of Deception, Confusion and Mind Control
- The Spirit of Mental Disorder
- The Spirit of Infirmity
- The Spirit of Poverty & Lack
- The Spirit of Perversion
- The Spirit of Parasite

However, there may be a more exhaustive list that you can relate to in your personal life or ministry. In addition, they can work alone as well as in groups or clusters. Please note that many of these unclean spirits have been previously defined in Chapter Fourteen under the area of STRONG MEN.

EXPOSING SPIRITS
(Functions, Characteristics, Manifestations, Affiliations and Mannerisms of Demonic Spirits)

**These are only a few of the many demonic spirits in operation in the earth realm. Many of these spirits become doorkeepers, and some of them can become strong men in your life to keep you bound. They can be grouped in chains and clusters, because many of them are similar in nature.

~∞⊙⑥∞~

The Spirit of Rebellion

The function of this spirit, along with its demonic counterparts, is to cause individuals to rebel against authority and established order in governments, churches, organizations, and families. This spirit influences people to be deliberately disobedient to authority, stubborn and defiant.

Some of the spiritual manifestations of people operating in a spirit of rebellion are:

☐ The spirit of **Leviathan:** this is a principality of satan and is known as the "captain of the snake brigade". It appears in forms as a spiny water spirit, crocodile, alligator, huge sea snake or dragon. It does not want to break or bow and is characterized by hardness of heart.
☐ The spirit of **Lawlessness:** disobedience, disorder, unruliness and rebellion.
☐ A **Wall Out spirit:** builds up barriers; not allowing others to get close
☐ The spirit of **Disloyalty:** a lack of commitment; lack of faithfulness
☐ **The spirit of Absalom:** seduction, pride, self-destruction; working in ministries to undermine pastors or those in authority.

180

Some of the behavioral manifestations in individuals may include:

- Bitterness
- Unruliness
- Anti-submissiveness
- Defensiveness
- Resistance
- Insubordination
- An "Unteachable" spirit
- Anger/Rage
- Strong-willed
- Contentious
- Hateful/Strife
- "Gangster" mentality

The Spirit of Pride

The function of this spirit, along with its demonic counterparts, is to cause individuals to operate in a self-gratifying, self-indulging, self-important and self-willed mindset. This spirit influences people to be arrogant, conceited, selfish and self-centered.

Some of the spiritual manifestations of people operating in a spirit of pride are:

- The spirit of **Pretense:** putting on a façade or make belief
- The spirit of **Intellectualism:** pride, knowledge and reasoning.
- The spirit of **Envy:** desiring or coveting what someone else has
- The spirit of **Jealousy:** spitefulness, bitterness or intense dislike for someone or something because of what they have or because you do not possess what they have
- The spirit of **Vanity:** Ego, pride, self-love.
- The spirit of **Offense:** Feelings of annoyance, disgust displeasure, resentment, indignation
- The spirit of **Leviathan** (See *REBELLION*)

Some of the behavioral manifestations in individuals operating in a spirit of pride may include:

- Haughtiness
- Defensiveness
- Disrespect
- Self-Protection
- Stinginess
- Self-Righteousness
- Negative
- Religious
- Intellectual
- Critical
- Scornful
- Deception

The Spirit of Anger

The function of this spirit, along with its demonic counterparts, is to cause individuals to go into a state of rage or literally lose control. This would include losing control of their mind, their speech, their emotions or their actions.

Some of the spiritual manifestations of people operating in a spirit of anger are:

☐ **The spirit of Murder:** unforgiveness, anger, revenge and retaliation

☐ **The** spirit of **Hatred:** operates with the spirit of dislike, hostility, racism and bitterness.

☐ The spirit of the **Panther:** violence, savagery, fierceness, "wildcat" behavior

☐ The spirit of **Resentment:** , unforgiveness, bitterness, rage, murder, envy, annoyance.

☐ The spirit of **Treachery:** cruelty, hatred, pride, jealousy.

☐ The spirit of **Violence:** rage, fury, retaliation; out-of-control behavior, confrontational

☐ The spirit of **Rage:** anger, fury.

Some of the behavioral manifestations in individuals may include:

- Loud, violent outbursts

182

- Irrational behavior
- Unreasonable (or unable to be reasoned with)
- Use of profanity
- Mental or physical abuse
- Retaliation

The Spirit of Abandonment

The function of this spirit, along with its demonic counterparts, is to cause individuals to withdraw from not only marital covenants but, also, from their duties and responsibilities in the kingdom. This spirit influences people to totally remove themselves from commitments to family, church and their jobs.

Some of the spiritual manifestations of people operating in a spirit of abandonment are:

☐ **The spirit of Demas:** this spirit manifests in the form of abandonment, neglect and confusion. It will cause you to abort your kingdom assignment. *(2 Timothy 4:10)*

☐ **The spirit of Orpah**: this spirit will cause you to leave the church; it will cause you to feel neglected and abandoned. *(Ruth 1:14 – 15)*

The Spirit of the Occult/Witchcraft

The function of this spirit, along with its demonic counterparts, is to cause individuals to worship the creation or creature rather than God, the Creator of all things. Individuals involved in any such practice normally become entangled, either by their curiosity about or the demonstration of 'false powers'. These ungodly practices

183

involve the perpetual use of familiar spirits to gain control and manipulate someone's life and destiny.

Some of the spiritual manifestations of people operating in the spirit of the occult/witchcraft are:

☐ **Familiar spirit:** this spirit has been assigned to observe and learn the hereditary behaviors of a family; it gathers information and becomes acquainted with all of the issues, behaviors and characteristics of the family which are carried from one generation to another. In turn, these spirits confer with witches, relaying this information to them. Eventually, these spirits literally become your friend, making it more difficult for deliverance workers to cast them out.

☐ **The spirit of Baal:** meaning possessor, lord, owner; drunkenness, lust, debauchery; also linked to the spirit of Ashtoreth.

☐ **The spirit of Ashtoreth:** the fertility goddess/ female deity of Baal that also promotes or encourages debauchery, sensuality, lust, drunkenness.

Some of the practices which are tied to the spirit of the occult include, but are not limited to:

- Astrology or Stargazing (eg. Horoscope, signs of the zodiac, and more)
- Palm reading
- Crystal gazing
- Divination
- Fire walking
- Hypnosis
- Levitation
- Fortune telling
- Psychic reading

SPECIAL NOTE

After witches, mediums and other persons operating in the spirit of the occult have consulted with familiar spirits, they now have access to "inside" information. This information is used to lead you to believe that they possess supernatural knowledge and power. It is important to understand that practicing or consulting with the occult will open doors to sickness, pain and a life of torment.

The Spirit of Addiction

The function of this spirit, along with its demonic counterparts, is to cause individuals to become hopelessly entangled through their compulsive needs or desires. It creates an erroneous mindset that you cannot do without something or someone. Further, this spirit causes an individual to develop habit forming tendency towards various substances or behaviors such as: drugs, alcohol, sex, pornography, food, work or career. These controlling spirits may lodge in the stomach, mouth, appetite, taste buds and nose.

Some of the spiritual manifestations of people operating in a spirit of addiction are:

☐ The spirit of **Abuse:** Compulsion or obsession for lethal substances, habits, behaviors such as: drugs, alcohol, nicotine, caffeine, sex and food.

☐ **A Lying Spirit (The spirit of deception):** A compulsion to mislead other that is attached to the spirit of deception

Some of the behavioral manifestations may include:
- Obsessive-compulsive disorders (OCD);
  (eg. Extreme addiction to repeated behaviors due to fear, anxiety, or some erroneous belief; creates an addiction to eating strange items such as rocks, paper, plastic, cotton, powder, deodorant, grass, raw flour, etc.)
- Addictions to abuse/pain
- Addictions to poverty
- Addictions to video games
- Addiction to garbage (Eg. Hoarders)
- Addiction to the Internet, Social Media, Technology
- Fatal Attractions/Stalking
- Eating disorders (eg. Gluttony, binging – alcohol, junk food, and more)
- Sexual perversion
- Gambling
- Excessive Computer games
- Excessive Television Viewing
- Obsession with Success
- Overworking (Work-a-holic)

The Spirit of Sabotage

The function of this spirit, along with its demonic counterparts, is to cause individuals to hinder, stifle, manipulate or destroy the lives of others, churches, families or organizations. Through mal-intent or the desire for personal gain, people operating in this spirit will seek to subvert or undermine the life of another person

Some of the spiritual manifestations of people operating in a spirit of sabotage are:
- ☐ The spirit of **Accident:** This spirit causes casualty, calamity, injury, misfortune.

☐ The spirit of **Divorce:** A covenant-breaking spirit that operates in hardness and separation; and may cause fear, rejection and hurt, and infertility in women.

☐ The spirit of **Suffocation:** A strangling, smothering spirit that chokes life out of individuals, visions, ideas, dreams, goals, assignments, and the like.

☐ The spirit of **Abortion:** This spirit will sabotage and destroy visions, leading people to abandon their assignment and purpose. It works with spirits of murder and miscarriage, causing premature termination of fetus. It works with the spirit of Molech in the areas of adultery, hatred and destruction of children and death.

Some of the behavioral manifestations may include:
- Constant confusion
- Misunderstandings/miscommunications
  (ie. especially of vital information)
- Constant malfunction, misplacement and destruction of equipment and other resources
- Inability to complete projects
- Forgetfulness/Loss of memory
- Apathy or loss of interest
- Indifference
- Slothfulness
- Opposition

The Spirit of Fear

The function of this spirit, along with its demonic counterparts, is to hinder, stagnate and prevent the development, growth, progress and ultimately the success of an individual or group of person such as a church or business. The spirit of fear works as an unusual feeling of threat or intimidation.

187

Some of the spiritual manifestations of people operating in a spirit of fear are:

- The spirit of **Anxiety:** fright, panic, alarm, terror
- The spirit of the **Phantom:** nightmare and delusion.
- The spirit of **Phobia:** irrational fear, horror and panic.
- The spirit of **Insecurity:** low self-esteem, self-doubt and timidity.
- The spirit of **Nightmare:** fear of darkness, terror by night (nighttime visitations by the perverted spirits: incubus and succubus.)
- The spirit of **Doubt:** this spirit operates in skepticism, hardness of heart and unbelief.
- The spirit of **Restlessness:** Worry, anxiety, impatience, nervousness.
- The spirit of **Stress:** anxiety, tension, worry, nervous breakdown.
- The spirit of **Shame:** feelings of guilt or embarrassment: operates strongly with religious spirits, self-condemnation, low self-esteem and unworthiness

Some of the behavioral manifestations may include:

- Self-doubt
- Unwillingness to try something new
- Fear of failure
- Excuses
- Timidity
- Lack of self-confidence or Low self-esteem
- Inability to trust
- Obsessive Compulsive Disorders (OCD): extreme behaviors which are motivated by the spirit of fear. For example, fear of germs, disease, height, the dark, of being alone, failure, success, loss, death and the like. Hypochondriacs suffer from a psychological condition which is a form of OCD where they worry

about having a sickness or disease but the illness is not medically verifiable.

The Spirits of Torment and Pain

The function of these spirits, along with their demonic counterparts, is to inflict constant physical, emotional, mental, financial or marital anguish on individuals through the use of past hurts, rejection, disappointments, uncertainties and other negative experiences.

Some of the spiritual manifestations of people operating in spirits of torment and pain are:

- The spirit of **Hurt:** being wounded by someone (mentally, emotionally or physically)
- The spirit of **Bitterness:** distaste, difficulty in accepting; causing sharp physical or mental pain or discomfort
- The spirit of **Pain:** torment or agitation caused by mental and physical anguish, such as: migraines, spasms and back pains.
- The spirit of **Oppression:** excessive pressure, burdens, torment and strain.
- The spirit of **Trauma:** turmoil, anguish, shock, accident.
- The spirit of **Suicide: defeat, depression, despair** hopelessness, self-destruction
- The spirit of **Grief:** this spirit operates in distress, sorrow and broken-heartedness.

Some of the behavioral manifestations of people operating in spirits of torment and pain may include:

- Instability
- Hopelessness
- Sadness
- Bitterness
- Self-condemnation
- Guilt
- Regret

The Spirit of Rejection

The function of this spirit, along with its demonic counterparts, is to permanently scar or discourage an individual in order to totally divert them from their God-given assignment.

Some of the spiritual manifestations of people operating in a spirit of rejection are:

- ☐ The spirit of **Frustration:** disappointments; stress, prevention from attaining or fulfilling a desire
- ☐ The spirit of **Indifference:** unconcerned or lackadaisical attitude, insensitivity, apathy
- ☐ The spirit of **Loneliness:** isolation, discouragement and dejection.

Some of the behavioral manifestations may include:

- Sorrowfulness
- Indecisiveness
- Jealousy
- Over Protectiveness
- Wall Out (Isolating Oneself)
- Blaming/Accusation
- Self-condemnation/Self-Pity
- Suspicion/Inability to trust
- Disappointment
- Lack of confidence
- Low self-esteem
- Envy

The Spirit of Arrested Development

The function of this spirit, along with its demonic counterparts, is to stifle the growth of an individual, group, church or organization.

Some of the spiritual manifestations of a person operating in a spirit of arrested development are:

- ☐ **Spiritual Blindness:** spiritual dullness, lack of vision; the inability to see in the realm of the spirit or perceive

☐ The spirit of **Passivity:** laziness, heaviness, slumber and idleness

☐ The spirit of **Paralysis:** disability, palsy, stroke and crippling

☐ The spirit of **Laziness:** slothfulness, sleepiness and drowsiness.

☐ The spirit of **Palsy:** disfiguring or contorting the spine, atrophy and cerebral palsy

☐ The spirit of **Bondage:** inability to move forward or advance

☐ The spirit of **Arrested Development:** prevention from maturing into adulthood: hindrance, obstruction of the personality, immaturity, and infantility, adolescence

☐ The spirit of **Slothfulness:** laziness or idleness

☐ The spirit of **Lethargy:** slowness, sluggishness and heaviness

☐ The spirit of **Hindrance:** to arrest, delay, stop or obstruct

☐ The spirit of **Retardation:** handicap, impediment

☐ The **"Bible" spirit:** this spirit will block and hinder people from reading and understanding the Bible

☐ The spirit of the **Vagabond:** restlessness, aimlessness, wandering, nomadic behavior

Some of the behavioral manifestations may include:
- Forgetfulness
- Difficulty comprehending
- Loss of Memory
- Spiritual Deafness, Dumbness, Blindness
- Insensitivity
- Lack of Retention
- Remedial Tendencies
- Spiritual Slothfulness
- Repeated Cycles of Behavior

The Spirits of Deception, Confusion and Mind Control

The function of these spirits, along with their demonic counterparts, is to deceive, dissuade or wrongfully influence an individual. Examples include the spirits of the octopus and squid. These demonic spirits possess tentacles which seek to suction or "snatch" people away from the things of God. This attack comes to the mind.

Some of the spiritual manifestations of people operating in deception, confusion and mind control are:

- The spirit of **Manipulation:** being overtaken or exploited by someone else
- The spirit of **Mind control:** confusion, mental pressure, hypnosis
- The spirit of **Deception:** being misleading
- The spirit of **Belial:** a conspiring, deceptive spirit
- The spirit of **Hypocrisy:** self-deception, being double minded
- The spirit of **Licentiousness:** overindulgence, excess, wickedness and corruption.
- The spirit of the **Octopus/Squid:** seducing spirits which operate in mind control, mental torment
- The spirit of the **Serpent:** viper, subtlety, slyness; the spirit of leviathan.
- The spirit of the **Python:** suppression, control and manipulation to the point where lifeblood is squeezed out of individuals, relationships, organizations, churches and the like
- The spirit of **Confusion:** mind battles, memory loss/forgetfulness, disorientation, frustration, lack of focus, distraction and inconsistency
- The **Stronghold spirit:** ruling spirit, rebellion and resistance to change
- The spirit of **Strife:** argumentativeness, contention, discord, disagreement
- The spirit of the **Siren:** a seducing spirit used to lure men to their destruction

☐ The spirit of the **Mind Witches:** exert an unusual and overpowering control over the mind of an individual

☐ The **Ekron** spirit: an intellectual spirit which promotes excessive reasoning; it also misleads or misguides you into relying on natural or carnal wisdom

Some of the behavioral manifestations may include:
- Slander
- Gossiping
- Lies/Distortion of the truth
- Character Assassination
- Ungodly Soul ties
- Manipulation

The Spirit Of Mental Disorder

The function of this spirit, along with its demonic counterparts, is to undermine an individual's God-given abilities and mental function.

Some of the spiritual manifestations of people operating in a spirit of mental disorder are:

☐ **Lunatic spirit:** erratic, irrational, inconsistent thinking and behavior

☐ The spirit of **Insanity:** madness, deranged and confused behavior

☐ The spirit of **Mental Dysfunction:** confusion, paranoia, bi-polar disorders and madness.

☐ The spirit of **Schizophrenia:** Double-mindedness, suicidal tendencies, self-rejection, unteachable and possessive attitude.

☐ **Bipolar** Spirit/Disorders: extreme mood swings

Some of the behavioral manifestations may include:
- Derangement
- Irrational thoughts
- Memory loss
- Nervousness
- Irrational Decisions
- Uncontrollable emotions
- Mistrust of People
- **Bi-polar Disorders

** There are a number of additional behavioral manifestations of an individual who is under the oppression of a bi-polar spirit. Such manifestations include, but are not limited to:

- Extreme mood swings
- Emotionally distraught
- Instability
- Inconsistency
- Extreme irritability
- Bursts of Anger/Impulsivity
- Unexplainable acute depression
- Suicidal tendencies
- Separation Anxiety
- Gross Mistrust of People

The Spirit of Infirmity

The function of this spirit, along with its demonic counterparts, is to afflict the body with sickness and disease.

Some of the spiritual manifestations of people under the attack of a spirit of infirmity are:

- The spirit of **Disorders:** a mental of physical malfunction
- The spirit of **Sickness:** failing health
- The spirit of **Disease:** an extended sickness which brings physical destruction or dysfunction to the mind or body

194

□ The spirit of **Afflictions:** discomfort and hardship which are placed upon you due to other people, situations, circumstances or experiences

Some manifestations of the spirit of infirmity may include:

- Blood disease
- Heart disease
- Asthma
- Diabetes
- High Blood Pressure/ Hypertension
- Cancer
- Anemia
- Feminine Disorders (Fibroids, Lumps,...)
- Masculine Disorders (Prostate Cancer,...)
- Arthritis
- Unexplainable Illnesses
- Recurring Illnesses

The Spirits of Poverty and Lack

The function of these spirits, along with their demonic counterparts, is to keep an individual in spiritual, financial or social bondage. Further, this spirit seeks to keep people void of what is necessary to meet a specific or recurring need.

Some of the spiritual manifestations of a person under the influence of spirits of poverty and lack are:

□ The spirit of **Insufficiency:** never having enough to meet or fulfill a need or demand

□ The spirit of **Barrenness:** causes un-productiveness, sterility and uselessness; it comes in as the result of a curse

□ The spirit of **Stinginess:** causes you to withhold your giving and justify your lack of giving

Some of the behavioral manifestations may include:

- Abject poverty
- Impropriety
- Insufficiency
- Hardship
- Shame
- Unbelief/Doubt
- A "Slack" Hand

- Financial Debt
- Infertility
  (eg. impotence,
  sterility)

The Spirit of Perversion

The function of this spirit, along with its demonic counterparts, is to persuade individuals to deviate from God's divine standards for righteous and holy lifestyles.

Some of the spiritual manifestations of a person bound by a spirit of perversion are:

SEXUAL PERVERSIONS
- ☐ The spirit of **Adultery:** sexual relations outside of marriage and works with the spirit of Jezebel and operates through spirits of lust.
- ☐ The spirit of **Prostitution:** sexual abuse, whoredom and harlotry
- ☐ The spirit of **Fornication:** sex before marriage
- ☐ The spirit of **Promiscuity:** lewdness, lust, fornication, perversion and sexual impurity
- ☐ The spirit of **Masturbation:** self-abuse, fantasy, self-defilement and self-gratification
- ☐ The spirit of **Lust:** inordinate passions, longing, excessive sexual desires, ungodly desire for position and power
- ☐ The spirit of **Whoredom:** perversion, seduction, rape, prostitution
- ☐ The **Transvestite spirit:** cross dressing, gender reassignment
- ☐ The spirit of **Pornography:** exposure to sexually explicit images; may cause marriages to split.
- ☐ The spirit of **Lewdness:** self-indulgence, carnality and debauchery
- ☐ The spirit of **Incest:** sexual relations with relatives

- ☐ The spirit of **Molestation:** inappropriate fondling, rape, forced sexual activity of any kind
- ☐ The spirit of **Homosexuality:** sexual relations with the same gender
- ☐ The spirit of **Sexual impurity:** Homosexuality, bestiality, incest, pornography
- ☐ The **Incubus:** a spirit that comes upon you during sleep and has sexual intercourse with women. This attack may come during the day or night.
- ☐ The **Succubus:** a demon spirit that comes in female form to have sexual intercourse with men during their sleep.
- ☐ The spirit of **Impurity:** a spirit that operates in perverted thoughts, lewdness and idolatry.
- ☐ The spirits of **Moab and Ammon:** spirits of perversion and incest.
- ☐ The spirit of **Uncleanness:** lewdness, sexual impurity, immorality and the like
- ☐ The spirits of **Sodom and Gomorrah:** spirits of homosexuality, perversion
- ☐ **Seducing/Luring spirits:** spirits which come after you with enticements, things pleasing to the eye, ears, mouth, etc. in an effort to draw you away from the things of God

OTHER PERVERSIONS – Some of the other non-sexual manifestations of the spirit of perversion are as follows:

- ☐ The spirit of **Obsession:** inordinate affection, domination, preoccupation with people, things, thoughts, conceit
- ☐ The spirit of **Obscenity:** profanity, filthiness, vulgarity, filthy conversation and cursing
- ☐ The spirit of **Immorality:** dishonorable conduct; not operating in the attitude or spirit of what is right

197

- The spirit of **Murmuring:** faultfinding, accusation and complaining which is intended to undermine progress
- The spirit of **Mammon:** corruption, love of money and filthy lucre
- The **"Pig" Spirit:** self-indulgence, greed

Some of the behavioral manifestations of the spirit of perversion may include:

- Unnatural affections
- Filthy thoughts
- Lewd Lust
- Fetishism
- Impure motives
- Seduction
- Unethical dealings

The Spirit of The Parasite

The function of this spirit along with its demonic counterparts is to literally "suck" the very life of an individual, group or organization, seeking only to benefit itself.

Some of the spiritual manifestations of people operating in the spirit of the parasite may include:

- The spirit of the **Parasite:** strong dependency, manipulation and control for personal gain or benefit, begging, misleading
- The spirit of the **Leech:** a sucking spirit which takes from you or takes advantage of you and gives nothing back
- The spirit of the **Tick:** sucks from you and brings spiritual contamination

Some of the behavioral manifestations may include:
- Strong dependency
- Lack of reciprocity
- Hoarding
- Leeching behavior
- Vampirism

Jesus died so that you can have power over all the powers of the enemy. You do not have to tolerate any demonic spirit operating in your life; once you identify which spirit is in operation, you can bind it and cast it out of your life, in Jesus' name. *(Luke 10:19)*

PART III

BREAKING THE CHAINS

CHAPTER SIXTEEN

~∞⧉∞~

THE FIGHT FOR YOUR SOUL: BINDING THE STRONG MAN

IDENTIFYING DEMONIC STRONGHOLDS

Unclean/demonic spirits and strong men spirits have names and can easily be identified by their counterparts – strongholds. Strongholds represent belief systems consisting of ideas and ideologies that may govern an individual, groups of people, small communities or even entire nations.

Strongholds can be defined in both the natural (physical) and spiritual realms. They can also be divinely or demonically inspired. Naturally, strongholds are used by the military as protection. However, spiritually, they are hiding places or crevices in a person's life for demonic/unclean spirits to conceal themselves.

The divine or God-inspired strongholds are realized when you reach a place of spiritual maturity where you see God as your fortress, deliverer, and strong tower. *(Psalm 18:2-3; Psalm 118:5-24; Proverbs 18:10).*

A stronghold can also be demonic in nature and totally orchestrated by satan, himself. The demonic strongholds usually affect individuals by attacking their mind or emotions with false arguments, which seek to spiritually demobilize and paralyze their thought patterns. The battlefield is in the mind. Whoever gains control of your mind, will eventually gain control of your life.

Many of the demonic strongholds that wage savage attacks against the mind are demonic spirits of the octopus or squid, mind witches, the spirit of the siren and others.

Strongholds are demonic agents assigned to keep you in bondage. In order for you to walk in total deliverance, you must first dismantle the stronghold, identify the strong man, bind him and cast him out. Some of the more common strongholds that I have encountered during ministry were:

- *Depression*
- *Anger*
- *Abuse*
- *Fear*
- *Rejection*
- *Self-hatred*

Even, though there are many entry points for demons, the strongholds give demonic spirits the reasons or the "legal right" to stay in your life. *(See more on entry points later in this Chapter)* For example, when a young woman has been raped she may, over a period of time, become very angry. This anger develops into rage and may eventually turn into a hatred for men.

Unless the stronghold of rape is dismantled then the stronghold of anger will cause her to replay the experience over and over again in her mind. The function of the strongman of anger is to keep her chronically angry. Thus, the stronghold of sexual abuse (rape) has opened the door for the destructive strongman of anger to seize her life and keep her in bondage.

The Word of God says in *John 10:10*, *"the thief cometh not but for to steal, and to kill, and to destroy; (but Jesus says I am come that they might have life and that they might have it more abundantly."* If for some reason the enemy has invaded your life with tragedy, trauma or distress, you must aggressively fight to keep the enemy "under your feet" and defeated in your life.

DEMOLITION OF STRONGHOLDS

Remember, deliverance means to be set totally free (in your mind, body, soul, and spirit). To *demolish* is the act or process of wrecking or totally destroying. This action, itself, denotes an aggressive, violent, or hostile maneuver.

An individual may have been in bondage for such a long time that it takes an aggressive counter-maneuver to "break" them free from their chains of bondage. Much spiritual warfare and the assistance of a Minister, anointed to bring deliverance, will help the individual to become totally free from the yoke of the devil.

> In *2 Corinthians 10:4* it states, *"For the weapons of our warfare are not carnal but mighty through God to the pulling down of strongholds; Casting down imaginations and every high thing that exalteth itself against the knowledge of Christ.*

Demolishing strongholds over nations and regions involves a similar process however, a more aggressive maneuver may be required in order to dismantle them. Therefore, whatever mindset or atmosphere dominates a society or culture of people, that commonly held belief usually gives access to principalities to function over that area.

For example, some nations are under principality strongholds, which may function through spirits of poverty or violence that were brought on by various insurgents of cultic beliefs or practices. We can see the manifestation of various ruling principalities over some countries such as:

Country	Ruling Principality
Haiti	Occult
India	Idolatry
Lebanon	Terrorism/War/Violence
Germany	Drunkenness
France	Perversion
Iraq	Political Infiltrations

Once a stronghold has been destroyed and diminished, the demon spirit has nowhere to hide and the other weaker (or lower ranking) demons will leave at your command in Jesus' name. Fill every empty space by releasing the spirit of God along with the fruit of the Spirit to be at work in the individual's life, region, country or nation. *(See more in this Chapter)*

THE SPIRIT OF REJECTION

Rejection is the refusal to embrace, accept, consider or acknowledge someone or something. It is to decline, disregard, disqualify, or disallow something or someone for whatever reason. The *spirit of rejection* can come in and overtake an individual through open doors of perpetual abuse, neglect, hurt, and pain.

Some of the causes of the spirit of rejection in your life may be:
- an unwanted pregnancy (in this case, the child experiences rejection from the womb)
- a child being rejected from his father who doesn't want a child so he does not carry out his

responsibilities or negates his responsibilities and becomes delinquent
- social rejection because of race, intelligence level, economic status, obesity
- rejection in relationships such as friendships, families

People suffering from a spirit of rejection may begin to feel worthless, eventually rejecting others and even themselves. Eventually, this self-defeating sprit may cause you to "wall out" or begin to isolate yourself as you become bitter, angry or jealous of others.

In referring to Jesus, *Isaiah 53:3* it states that, *"He is despised and rejected of men; a man of sorrows, and acquainted with grief…he was despised and we esteemed Him not."*

As a result of the spirit of rejection working in your life, you begin to reject yourself and others. This is called self-rejection. You may experience or say things like, "If only I was prettier." "If only I had more money." "If only my nose was not so big." "If only I could lose weight."

Most people have experienced rejection at some point in time during the course of their lives. However, it is when you allow the hurt or pain of that rejection to permeate your soul that it may affect your will, intellect or emotions to the point that this spirit now manipulates, directs, and controls your life.

Therefore, most people who are under the spirit of rejection may find themselves being unaccepted, disqualified, moving from relationship to relationship, insecure about themselves and, for the most part, under constant abuse and ridicule from others, including their spouse. If the spirit of rejection is not broken off of your life, even your kindness, willingness to serve and forgiving nature may be taken for granted.

Signs and Symptoms of the spirit of Rejection

Anger	*Passive-Aggressiveness*
Over-Compensation	*Over-Sensitivity*
Depression/ Grief	*Fearfulness*
Self Pity	*Isolation*
Addictions	*Emotional Instability*
Insecurities	*Need for Approval*
Loneliness	*Mistrust/ Lashing Out*
Lack of Confidence	*Eating Disorders/Obesity*
Bitterness	*Perversion*

Many people are in a spiritual battle because the enemy uses every avenue or opportunity to keep them bound in their soul. He consistently seeks to wound or scar your soul by manipulating your personal associations through demonic soul ties, unhealthy relationships, adverse life experiences and more.

SOUL TIES

A soul tie is a spirit that has the ability to attract and unite people with like attitudes, tendencies and behaviors. It creates a connecting force between two individuals or entities for the purpose of the reinforcement of godly or ungodly interests. Some soul ties may begin as God-ordained relationships and may, for a time, fulfill His purpose.

However, if allowed, the enemy may come in and pervert the original intent for that relationship in order to accomplish his diabolical and sinful plans. Whenever this relationship becomes contaminated and is no longer God-centered then it can no longer bring glory to Him.

BREAKING THE CHAINS

TYPES OF SOUL TIES

There are various types of soul ties which may include:
- Sexual Soul Ties
- Diabolical Confederations (an association, union, link)
- Religious Soul Ties
- Covenant Soul Ties – marriage, business partnerships, etc.
- Ties of Allegiance (commitment)
- Ties of Alliance (treaty, pact, deal)
- Ties to families (such as, in-laws)
- Ties to demonic spirits (pain, rejection, shame, unforgiveness and more)
- Ties to organizations (lodges, fraternities, sororities, other secret orders/societies)

GODLY SOUL TIES

Godly soul ties point you toward your spiritual destiny. Each person involved in this relationship is able to give as well as receive. There is no form of manipulation, condemnation, or control. This relationship does not take you out of the will of God. Some people who demonstrated this type of godly relationship were Naomi and Ruth, David and Jonathan, and Elijah and Elisha.

Ruth and Naomi had more than a mother-in-law/daughter-in-law relationship. Ruth was deeply devoted and committed to Naomi, even when she had nothing to offer her. Ruth declared in *Ruth 1:16-17*:

"Entreat me not to leave thee,...for whither thou goest I will go and where thou lodgest, I will lodge: thy people shall be my people, and thy God, my God:"

David and Jonathan also demonstrated a kindred spirit of deep loyalty and respect. Jonathan was willing to protect David at all cost, even against his father, King Saul. According to **1 *Samuel* 20:17**, *"...for he loved him as he loved his own soul..."*. This covenant that David and Johnathan had with each other was rooted in love.

Further, Elisha and Elijah exemplified a godly soul tie. Elisha in **1 *Kings* 19**, desired to follow and serve Elijah, the man of God. He sacrificed his inheritance and declared with his own mouth that he would not break rank or look back because he realized that "looking back is death." As a result of his loyalty, Elisha was anointed with a mantle from Elijah and received a double portion of his spirit.

Godly soul ties are designed to help you become the person God intended you to be. We all need Naomis in our lives, spiritual mothers who help to birth us into our divine destiny. We all need Jonathans, who will be willing to sacrifice for us, even at the expense of denying self, privileges, and prestige. Finally, we all need Elijahs who are willing to mentor us and mold us so that we are equipped to function in our God-ordained purposes.

GODLY AND HEALTHY RELATIONSHIPS

In a godly relationship you should not be the only giver. Each person should be willing to give and receive. There is no manipulation or force.

Godly relationships will not violate your conscience or ask you to go against the will of God for your life. In a godly relationship, the other person is committed to your spiritual health and well-being; they are symbiotic in nature.

Symbiotic (Win-Win) Relationships

An example of healthy relationships is a symbiotic one where each individual is willing to give and receive. There is equal reciprocity in these types of relationships, which empowers both parties involved.

UNGODLY SOUL TIES

This type of relationship is characterized by a blatant, but sometimes subtle, element of manipulation and control. The "stronger" lords over the "weaker" and becomes a doorkeeper over the weaker person's life. The weaker individual then seeks affirmation to validate his self-worth and few decisions are made without the input of the "stronger", whether it concerns what to eat, wear or what to do with their finances.

The ultimate goal of ungodly soul ties is to distract and derail an individual, pulling him away from fulfilling his God-ordained purpose and kingdom assignment.

You must endeavor to sever ungodly soul ties or they will eventually lead to your destruction or eventual demise. Your soul cannot prosper if it is fragmented, in bondage or soul tied to anything, any place or anyone that does not line up with the will of God for your life. You must seek diligently to be delivered from such diabolical soul ties.

UNGODLY AND UNHEALTHY
RELATIONSHIPS

Ungodly or unhealthy relationships usually deplete the will, intellect, or emotions of one or both parties. These relationships generate ungodly and sometimes vicious cycles of abuse, mistrust, deception and frustration.

Any relationship that pulls you away from your God-ordained purpose or function is an ungodly relationship. Relationships that you find difficult, tiring, unproductive or draining are unhealthy relationships.

Individuals that you consider to be "high maintenance" fall into this category. God has called us to be "helpers of each other's joy." However, if you are in a relationship where you are giving of your time, your attention and your emotions but you are not getting a similar benefit from the other individual, then you may be in an unhealthy relationship. The Word of God reminds us in 3 John verse 2 that, above all else, it is God's desire for His people to prosper and be in good health even as their souls prosper.

Unhealthy, long-term relationships are a threat to the prosperity of your soul. Some examples of unhealthy and potentially dangerous relationships are parasitic, co-dependent and toxic relationships.

Parasitic (I-Win, You-Lose) Relationships

Parasites are known as organisms that depend on something else for their existence without making adequate contributions to the thing on which it depends. A parasitic relationship can be described as a relationship between two individuals where the "parasite", usually the weaker individual, benefits while harming the stronger individual. The weaker person seeks out an unusual amount of attention, instruction, affirmation and more from the stronger individual.

People who suffer from the spirit of low self-esteem, a lack or loss of identity and depression may become parasites in a relationship. It may be necessary that these individuals be delivered before entering any other type of relationship, whether platonic or intimate.

Co-dependent (I-Lose, You-Lose) Relationships

Co-dependent relationships develop out of a fear shared by both individuals that they are unable to live without each other. In this case both people suffer from low self-esteem and feel that they are incomplete. They enter relationships not out of love or care, but out of their own lack or sense of neediness.

For example, I have counseled many young women who have been abused throughout their entire life, beginning from their childhood. I have noticed that most of these women have married men that continue to abuse and mistreat them. The man, on the other hand, may be struggling with some form of addiction, be it drugs or sexual vices, such as: pornography, extra-marital affairs, pedophilia, etc.

Usually, she stays in the relationship for security because of her own lack of confidence and low self-esteem. On the other hand, he stays in the relationship because she allows him to take advantage of her which gives him a sense of strength and power. Although it appears that they are "looking out for each other", these relationships perpetuate unhealthy, vicious cycles where each person focuses on mitigating the other person's shortcomings, while ultimately hiding from their own issues.

Toxic (I-Lose, You-Lose) Relationships

These relationships are demonic and deadly. They are marked by violent and abusive behavior by either or both parties involved. Individuals in these relationships are sometimes characterized by being critical, chronic complainers who see wrong or evil in everything.

These toxic individuals endanger the lives of others, painfully killing them by spewing out abrasive words and, eventually, poisoning themselves by their own venom. These are, normally, blatant dream-killers who themselves, have achieved very little in life. We must be wary of such negative, fault-finding people who are pessimistic by nature.

If you find yourself in such a relationship, you should immediately sever all ties to this individual and seek to connect yourself with optimistic people who will celebrate, and not seek to sabotage, your purpose in life.

Please note that there are many types of relationships in life. However, the person you are will ultimately affect whether or not you maintain healthy or unhealthy relationships and ultimately influence your destiny.

The Dependent Person

Dependent people are always needy, leaning on the opinions of others. They are easily influenced by others, their circumstances or issues and find it difficult to stand on their own. Most dependent people find it difficult to make quick, sound, or resolute decisions. They are weak-minded people who are constantly in need of attention and affirmation.

Sometimes these people manifest spirits of low-self esteem, insecurity, timidity and passivity. An individual seeking to help dependent people should be someone who is seasoned and matured in the things of God. Some biblical examples of dependent people are Ahab and the man at the Pool of Bethesda *(John 5).*

The Independent Person

Independent people are people who feel as though they do not need anybody. They are self-willed, self-centered and tend to present themselves as though they know everything. They believe that everything they have achieved has been because of their own strength; they credit no-one else, not even God.

These individuals do whatever they want to do and are haughty, arrogant, and full of pride. They tend to "wall out" from others, are very unteachable and do not willingly accept suggestions or corrections.

The spirit of Jezebel loves independent people who are controlling, manipulating and overbearing. She subtly operates through them causing them to think more highly of themselves than they ought to think. It can be very difficult maintaining any kind of relationship with an independent person. Some biblical examples of independent people are: Naboth, Jezebel, Nebuchadnezzar, Herod, Haman and many others.

The Inter-dependent Person

The "healthy" balance between the dependent and the independent person is the inter-dependent person. This person is able to interact, work, function and socialize with others while maintaining a personal identity of his own. This type of person knows when to ask for help and knows when to intuitively and wisely initiate, resolve, and intervene in situations.

A relationship with an inter-dependent person may be one of the healthiest types of relationships. Some biblical examples of people who were inter-dependent are Ruth with Naomi, Elisha with Elijah and Paul with Timothy.

CHARACTER TRAITS

Some of the great philosophers, medical and spiritual leaders of early times have adopted various theories which they believe help to define human character traits. Whereas some of these findings may be factual, outside of the Spirit of God, no one test, instrument, evaluation and the like can comprehensively define who you really are as a person.

In other words, when you were in your mother's womb, God placed in you, the truest essence of your DNA and character, which ultimately defines who you will eventually become. The person that *you are* today is the sum total of what God has placed inside of you combined with what has happened to you in life. The person *you will become* tomorrow remains in the treasure of life's experiences and in the heart and mind of the One who created you.

Below is a list of innate character strengths and weaknesses which some people may possess:

Strength	*Weaknesses*
Efficient/Organized	Rigid and Unbendable
Disciplined	Overly Critical
Strong-willed	Intolerant & Impatient
Independent-Thinker	Easily Offended
Self-motivated	Self-Centered
Friendly/Easy going	Easily persuaded
Passionate	Disorganized
Sociable	Undisciplined
Creative	Extremely Negative
Compassionate	Easily Distracted
Humble	Procrastinator
Easy-going	Overly Confidential
Peacemaker	Unorganized
Detail-Oriented	Skeptical/Doubtful
Decisive	Unmotivated/Passive

There are over 6.8 billion people in the world and every one possesses character strengths and weaknesses. It is, therefore, vitally important to understand that without the intervention, regulation and guidance of the Holy Spirit, we would all succumb to our weaknesses.

CHAPTER SEVENTEEN

~≪⊙⊚⊙≫~

THE FIGHT FOR YOUR SOUL: GATEWAYS TO THE SOUL

ILLEGAL ACCESS

Demons cannot enter you without legal grounds or legal authorization to come in. Living a life of iniquity, holding onto articles or objects that are tied to the occult and having unprotected "gates" help to give them access.

There are several primary gates listed below. If these are left unprotected, demons seek to gain entrance into your life. These gateways to your soul include:

- *The MIND Gate:* you must be careful what you allow yourself to think; your thoughts eventually become actions, therefore you must not allow yourself to entertain ungodly thoughts

- *The EYE Gate:* pornography, horror movies, witnessing killings, and like influences

- *The NOSE Gate:* witchcraft potions, dust, drugs and perfumes can be inhaled if the person is not protected by the Blood of Jesus and living obedient to God.

- *The MOUTH Gate:* spirits can enter in through eating, drinking and even kissing. If the person is involved in witchcraft; they may kiss you deceitfully to put a curse on you, using their saliva as a point of contact for demons to transfer.

- *The SEX ORGANS:* sexual relations outside of marriage open the gate for demons to come in.

- *The EAR Gate:* you must be careful what you allow yourself to hear or you could open your ear gate to demons. (For example, rock music, seductive and lustful words, words of fear, hurt and intimidation.)

- *The PORES:* Just as an individual can be anointed with oil for godly purposes, so can a witch anoint for evil. Instead of healing taking place, sickness may occur; instead of strength, weakness, and so on.

In order for us to live a life of peace and harmony, we must guard and protect these entry points into our soul. The Bible warns that if you break the hedge, the serpent will bit you. Give no space to the devil, neither a foothold nor a space in your life. You must seek to do everything in your power to protect the *"gateways to your soul."*

OTHER DEMONIC ENTRY POINTS

If you are a born again believer, no demon has legal rights to enter and destroy your life unless you "open a door" or all them to have "areas of access" or entry points to your soul by engaging in any of the following:

- *Willful Sin – when you make a conscious decision to sin*

- *Fornication/Adultery – having sexual interaction with someone who is not your spouse*

- *Involuntary Inheritance – familiar spirits that are found in the bloodline (family line)*

- *Occult practices and artifacts – horoscopes, zodiac, charms, transcendental meditation, ouija boards, etc.*

- *Abandonment – when you are left suddenly and/or unexpectedly by a parent, spouse, loved one, or primary care-giver*

- *Addiction – an unhealthy or unnatural craving for something or someone (For example: sex, drugs, food, gambling, co-dependent or toxic relationships…)*

- *Abuse – the misuse of something or exploitation of someone; when you abandon the original use of a thing*

- *Generational curses, sins, and the like – ungodly practices, proclivities or habits which are common to your ancestors*

- *Ungodly alliances – when you come into agreement or covenant with someone that God did not ordain*

- *Rejection – when you are not accepted, included or validated*

- *Bitterness or Hatred, – if you harbor any malice or unforgiveness in your heart, you may eventually struggle with the spiritual contaminants of bitterness and hatred*

- *Hypnotism - the theory or practice of inducing a sleep-like condition for the purpose of retrieving information that lost or hidden in the mind*

- *Rebellion (against authority) – resistance and the refusal to submit, obey, or acknowledge established laws, rules, and guidelines*

- *Abortion – destruction of a fetus*

- *Childhood hurt and traumatic experiences*

- *Idolatry – worshiping anything or anyone other than God*

- *.. and more.*

God has given you power over all the powers of the enemy. This power has been given to you in the name of Jesus and by the blood that He shed on Calvary. Therefore, you possess the authority to regain control of your life. Whichever unclean spirits are in your life, they all have a point of reference and answer to a specific name. It is imperative that you address each spirit by name and verbally command them to leave your life. However, careful guidance or assistance should be given by a leader, Minister, or someone who is trained in this area.

SOUL SCARS AND SOUL WOUNDS

"The spirit of a man will sustain his infirmity; but a wounded soul who can bear?" (Proverbs 18:14)

God created man in His image and in His likeness. The spirit part of man belongs solely to God; it is immortal and eternal. Thus man was created to serve and worship the One and Only True God, Elohim.

The carnal or fleshly part of Man was created as a suit to house man's spirit and soul. The soul, on the other hand, deals with the will, the intellect (the mind), and the emotions. Thus, the soul is who you really are.

Therefore, the more you feed your soul spiritual things, the more spiritual you will become. On the other hand, the more you feed your soul carnal things, the more carnal you become as a person.

All of our five senses affect our soul. The decisions we make on a daily basis, whether we are happy or sad and even the way we think, all comes out of our soul. The soul is the seat of our feelings and emotions, our personality; the soul is the essence of who we really are.

When a baby is conceived in the womb of its mother, all of the basic characteristics such as his personality, individuality, uniqueness, distinctiveness have already been pre-determined and pre-destined by God. These unique traits are there to identify who that child would look like, talk like, act like, and so on.

In *Jeremiah 29:11* the word of the Lord declares, *"For I know the thoughts that I think towards you, saith the Lord, thoughts of peace and not evil, to give you an expected end [future]"*. From the very beginning of life, even before we

223

were formed in our mother's womb, God had a plan for our lives.

The Bible further declares in 3 John verse 2, *"I wish above all things that you may prosper and be in good health even as your soul prospers."* There are, however, some traits which a child will inherit from its family lineage. These can be generational blessings or generational curses. *(See more later in this Chapter)*

The enemy of our soul, *"the devil"* desires to kill, steal and destroy us even from birth or while we are in our mothers' womb. Many mothers endure extremely difficult and even distressing ordeals during pregnancy and may experience physical abuse, financial challenges and even consider abortion, suicide and the like. These feelings, in many cases, are passed down to us and are seen in our lives as we begin to grow up from childhood to adulthood.

I have been privileged to travel and preach the gospel in many countries around the world. During these travels I have noticed that some of the same issues remain constant in the body of Christ. In almost all of the congregations, more than three quarters of the people suffered from the spirits of hurt, pain, rejection, guilt, shame, and condemnation.

The Holy Spirit began to speak to me and show me that many people in the kingdom of God were still suffering from soul wounds and soul scars that had never been healed. Because of these neglected wounds, many are unable to sit still long enough in order to stabilize themselves in God.

Can you picture being bitten by a vicious dog and rushed to the hospital where the only thing they did was wrap the wounds in bandages and send you back home? Or could you imagine receiving second to third degree burns but there is no ointment in the hospital to treat your wounds and, therefore, you are sent home to wait until a certain amount of time passes until your wounds heal and eventually become scars? Although these scars no longer hurt, they, however remind you of the horrifying ordeal you have just survived, while you are told to simply "get over it and move on!"

Believe it or not, that is exactly what happens in churches every day. People come rushing to conferences and church meetings bleeding and falling apart from old wounds and scars to their soul. For the most part they are regarded as just another number in the pew. The pastor, in some cases has never been healed of his soul wounds from the past so he is hardened and insensitive to the cries of those who are presently in pain and does not know how to deal with them.

LEAKING ISSUES

As we go along life's way, we come in contact with others and forge relationships with people from our neighborhoods, schools, churches, jobs or other places. We are constantly challenged with being affected and even afflicted in our souls. In some shape or form, our souls are negatively or positively tied to something or someone. *Proverbs 4:23* says that we must *keep [guard] our heart* [soul] *with all diligence for out of it flows the issues of life.*

Sometimes we experience situations that we had not anticipated. On the other hand, some behaviors that we now manifest are due to hereditary tendencies, propensities, traits, personalities and other mannerisms that were passed down from one generation to another or represent personal things we experienced but were never healed. *(See more in this chapter on Generational/Ancestral Curses)*

For example, some grandparents may have lived promiscuous lives. Therefore, the tendency towards promiscuity is ultimately passed down to ensuing generations. Such practices which may include adultery, fornication, lying, stealing, deception, and other practices which were considered to be a normal, everyday lifestyle.

Therefore, when you were born and began to forge your own personal relationships, you found yourself repeating these negative behaviors which, eventually, caused vicious, destructive cycles to develop in your life. Because you were not taught otherwise, you ignorantly got involved in one promiscuous relationship after another, not realizing that you were leaving pieces of your soul with each person you were connected with and your soul was becoming fragmented.

For the most part, many of these relationships were destructive because the people to whom you have given yourself may have, themselves, suffered through a similar vicious cycle of fornication, lust, adultery, sexual abuse and other negative experiences. This now forms a diabolical or destructive relationship or an ungodly soul tie. Remember, hurting people sometimes hurt other people.

When these relationships end, pieces of the soul are left behind, another soul-wound develops and your soul (mind, will, intellect, and emotions) continues to "bleed." These wounds are invisible to the naked eye but are evidenced in how we manage everyday relationships.

THE TRAUMATIZED SOUL

Many people have experienced various devastating events or unhealthy relationships which have literally left their souls traumatized. Unfortunately, they have never been properly healed from the hurt of these past experiences or broken relationships, which have left them vulnerable or fearful of trusting or loving others again.

As a result of this fear, people who have been deeply wounded or hurt find it extremely difficult to trust others, fearing that they will be wounded again. They sometimes reject necessary, healthy relationships and attach themselves to unhealthy ones that perpetuate the same abuses. This fear keeps them isolated, lonely and deprived of healthy relationships that are necessary for the healing of their soul.

In some cases, soul scars and wounds may result in memory loss. If left unchecked the pain, hurt and rejection which affect us deep in our souls would leave painful scars and wounds, resulting in the development of various demonic strongholds.

If a child is sexually molested or left to himself without food or shelter this will, no doubt, leave a scar in the soul of that child. He may grow up acting out in ways that he would not want to because of spirits of rejection and abandonment which have become rooted in his soul. If these demonic strongholds of rejection and abuse are not recognized by someone who understands and knows how to deal with them, he may find himself continually acting out in these self-destructive behaviors.

FRAGMENTS OF YOUR SOUL

For some people, deep-rooted soul scars and wounds have been so entrenched in their souls that they become comfortable and we do not want or even know how to let go of these past hurts.

By the time they find the right mate, they are so messed up in their souls that they are not able to give themselves wholeheartedly to the one they love. If they are ever going to fully embrace new relationships, the must seek to be delivered and totally set free so that the "fragments" of their soul can be put back together.

God wants you to be whole. *1 Thessalonians 5:23* says *"And the very God of peace sanctify you wholly; and I pray God your whole spirit and soul and body be preserved blameless..."*

From the very foundation of this world God had placed His spirit inside of mankind. God breathed into man's nostrils and man became a living soul (*Genesis 2:7*). We were made whole and complete in Christ Jesus. (*Colossians 2:10*)

IDENTIFYING SOUL SCARS AND SOUL WOUNDS
"How Do you Know That You Have
Soul Wounds and Soul Scars?"

There are many signs which indicate that you have soul wounds and soul scars. A primary example can be in the case of child abuse. There are many people who have been abused as children, either verbally, physically or, worst of all, sexually.

Although these persons grow into adulthood you will immediately see traits of anger, rage, pain, hurt, resentment, wall out, guilt, shame, distrust, or violent outbursts when placed in the same or similar situations. For others, even the slightest memory of such incidents can trigger or evoke a number of negative emotions. These people sometimes go through life abusing others and even themselves.

Many children experience what psychologists call separation anxiety. This happens when there is a tragic occurrence in the life of a child and he or she is immediately separated from the primary care-giver or nurturer.

If the incident is not resolved in a child's mind, he can become fearful, angry, confused, timid, or withdrawn, which can follow him all the way to adulthood if these traumatic incidences are never correctly resolved. Such events include, but are not limited to, sudden deaths, tragedies, accidents, destruction due to natural disasters (hurricanes, tornados, earthquakes, and more) or divorce.

I believe that when parents go through a separation or divorce that children go through it also. Parents should take the time to communicate with their children after major incidences have occurred in their lives or seek counseling for them.

Soul wounds are obvious in people's lives through their inabilities to truly love or trust again. Sometimes the wounds can be so deep that it is extremely difficult to even talk about the pain.

In cases of rejection or abandonment, many adults have problems coping with life even though the other party that was in the relationship moves on and continues on with his life. Most people suffering from soul wounds or scars in the form of hurt or pain from previous relationships hardly ever move on.

And if they do find themselves in another relationship it is normally with the same type of people that they had in their previous relationship.

Other behavioral symptoms of soul scars and soul wounds are:

- withdrawal
- memory loss
- self-abusive or self-destructive practices such as unprotected casual sex, Russian roulette and more
- relationship avoidance – the fear of becoming intimate or getting close to people again

OVERCOMING SPIRITS OF FEAR AND DOUBT

I can remember a season in my life when I struggled to overcome spirits of fear and doubt. I had experienced so much while growing up that I too had to deal with trauma to my soul.

Fear and doubt are tag team partners that I call twin demon spirits. Whenever you see one, the other is always present. Fear is simply false evidence that only appears to be real. It is like a man on a long, dark, lonely street late at night. He stands under a lamp pole and then takes off running only to discover later that there was no one behind him, it was just his shadow. The spirit of fear works like a smoke screen; once you turn on the light it eventually disappears.

"For God has not given us the spirit of fear; but of power, of love, and of a sound mind." (2 Timothy 1:7)

The spirit of fear is a subtle undermining agent of Satan. He can enter your life from birth or childhood and will manifest when you are about to do something great or something that would take your life to the next level. There are many people who live in constant fear every day of their lives. They are in fear of the dark, heights, elevators, escalators, dogs, death, failure, trusting people and the like.

I came to realize that all of these fears resulted from some negative experience these individuals had at some point in their lives, sometimes originating from experiences that go all the way back to childhood or infancy. If you are going to go to the next level, you must make a conscious decision to overcome and defeat these evil spirits.

It was at some of the most defining moments in my life that I can clearly remember receiving a visitation from them. They (fear and doubt) are very subtle and can be invisible to the naked eye. When they show up, they never announce their arrival by blowing a trumpet or saying, "We're here!" They simply burst on to the scene at the very moment you least expect.

The Dream That Opened My Eyes

A few years ago I went on a short sabbatical to seek God. On the third night I fell into a deep sleep and began to dream. I was standing on what appeared to be a very high mountain. Out of nowhere, two men flew out of the sky and landed beside me. They were very big and told me not to be afraid because they were sent from the presence of God to teach me how to fly. I looked at them in utter amazement because, not only did I not know how to fly, I did not have wings.

Then they turned back to me as if they could read my mind and said, "Here, put these on; they will help you to fly." Whatever they gave me was invisible to the naked eyes. However, I literally felt as if an anointing was being released upon me in the form of wings. The two men, angels as I now understand them to be, took off and began to soar high into the clouds. They shouted to me and said, "Come, now it is your time."

Just as I was about to move, I felt another presence behind me. This time it was two other men wearing black hoods, which I immediately discerned were demonic spirits. I could not see their faces. However, I'd never forget their voices. They spoke with a false, subtle piety, pretending to be concerned about my safety.

One of them said to me, "Oh my, oh my, Mattie. You are not *really* thinking about lifting off this mountain, are you?" The other man shoved me slightly forward and said, "Look at how high you are from the ground." He continued by saying, "It is so dangerous down there, and you may kill yourself!" The other two men – the angel beings - shouted from above to me saying, "Mattie, you can do this; it is easy, just try."

I was immediately thrust into a state of confusion and fear. On one hand, I felt like I was able to lift high off the mountain and fly. But on the other hand, I felt extremely afraid, doubtful and not to mention, powerless. What should have been a simple encounter broke out into an all out war between the demons of fear and doubt and the angels of faith and courage. To this day, I will never forget that experience. I remember literally lifting off the mountain and soaring to heights where I had never been.

Over the years the Lord has spoken to me through many dreams and visions. These dreams and visions have helped to steer me in the right direction. Whenever God is taking you to the next level or dimension you can expect visitations from fear and doubt in some shape or form. You must have the courage to break the chains of fear and doubt and do exactly what God is calling you to do.

In *1 John 4:18* it says, *"...perfect love casteth out fear:..."*. With the thought that Jesus loved me so much and that He would not allow anything bad to happen to me,

I lifted myself off the mountain and began to fly, leaving fear and doubt behind.

Confidence and Courage to Overcome

Confidence is knowing, without a shadow of a doubt, that God is able to do exceeding, abundantly above whatsoever you ask of Him. One of the only ways you will ever do great things in this life is to have faith and confidence in God.

> "...and this is the confidence we have in him
> that whatsoever we ask in His name, he will
> do it." (1 John 5:14-15)

> As it says in **Psalm 20:7**, "Some trust in [and
> boast of] chariots and some in horses; but we
> will trust in, [and boast of] the Lord our God."
> "They that trust in, [lean on, and confidently
> hope in] the Lord shall be as Mount Zion,
> which cannot be moved but abideth and stands
> fast forever. As the mountains are round
> about Jerusalem, so the Lord is round about
> His people..." (Psalm 125:1-2)

God will never leave you nor forsake you. He has built a hedge of protection around you. In order for the enemy to gain access to you, he *must* get permission.

Like Job, God has placed a spiritual electromagnetic field around your entire life. The only way satan gets in is if God allows him to or if we give him permission through sinful practices or generational curses. *(See Chapter 18 on Generational/Ancestral Curses.)*

Courage is the "can do" attitude that works with confidence. God told Joshua in Joshua 1:8 that Moses was dead but he was to be strong and very courageous. His courage was to be seen later on as he faced the fierce army of the Midianites.

These were "terrorists" that would fight to their death. Joshua knew that if the sun went down the Midianites would have defeated the army of Israel. So he exercised courage and commanded the moon to stand still over Ajalon and the sun to stay over Gibeon until the entire Midianite army was weakened and destroyed. (Joshua 10:12)

HOW TO RESTORE THE WOUNDED SOUL
Restoration of the Soul

The restoration of the soul is the bringing back of the soul (will, intellect, and emotions) to its original intended position in God. This is what it means to be complete and whole.

In *1 Thessalonians 5:23* it states, *"And the very God of peace sanctify you wholly; and I pray God your whole spirit and soul and body be preserved blameless unto the coming of our Lord Jesus Christ."*

David says in Psalm 23, *"...He restoreth my soul..."* (*See more in Chapter the area on The Ten Commandments of Receiving and Maintaining Your Deliverance*)

To survive as a believer you must break your soul ties with cults; the occult (including lodges, fraternities, sororities, and WICCA); ungodly relationships with ex-spouses, boyfriends, girlfriends or sexual partners and others who may have sought to dominate your life.

In order to restore a wounded soul, you must be prepared to:

- sever the cords or ties with people, places and/or organizations that may have negatively impacted you in the past
- through prayer, fasting, and spiritual warfare break strongholds in the mind and emotions that keep the soul-wounds from being healed
- seek godly and healthy relationships

PRAYER FOR BREAKING UNGODLY SOUL TIES

In the name of Jesus, I choose to put off the old creation. I put off any remaining soul ties with people in the past which would bind or hinder my Christian growth and walk.

I come against any such soul ties now. I reject them and put them off in the name and power of the blood of the Lord Jesus Christ, who is my victory, my sanctifier, separating me unto the Body of Christ into liberty, unto freedom.

I declare every soul tie that is not of the Lord to be broken. I renounce each one in the name of the Lord Jesus. I declare any such bondage to be over, because I am cleansed by the shed blood of Jesus and born again. His resurrection victory over the grave gives me power and authority over all things.

Satan, I declare myself to be loosed from you and all your demons. I declare myself to be bound only unto the liberated Body of Christ; to be knit together in love, in the glorious liberty of the children of God. I praise you, dear Lord, for You are the Lion of the tribe of Judah. You break every fetter and let the oppressed go free, and open the prison house of the captives, setting those free who were once held captive.

In the name of Jesus Christ, I break soul ties with the following; (now name specifically any person, group, organization, or thing that comes to mind). In the name of Jesus Christ, I declare myself free from all cords, bands, ties, and tentacles of soul ties and command all personality spirits of any other person or people to leave me now!! I decree and declare healing and deliverance from all soul wounds and soul scars.

I ask you, Lord Jesus, to dispatch the ministering spirits to bring back and restore any part of my fragmented soul that is attached to any group, person, or organization that is not of You; restore my soul and make me whole. I pray this prayer in Jesus' name. AMEN!

CHAPTER EIGHTEEN

THE POWER OF DELIVERANCE

DELIVERANCE DISCLAIMER

It is advised that you should not seek to administer deliverance unless you have been trained or otherwise directed by the Holy Spirit. Because the process of deliverance involves direct spiritual combat with satanic forces it should, therefore, not be entered into ignorantly or when ill-prepared as it can result in serious bodily injury or even the death of any individual involved.

THE POWER OF DELIVERANCE

Deliverance is a forward, upward mobility of coming into the revelation and knowledge of the truth of God concerning your life and spiritual well-being. Deliverance simply means to be totally set free. Further, it is the ability to increase your spiritual capacity by moving from one level to the next using spiritual discerment and the kingdom tools necessary to do so.

Deliverance is the removal of the mind, body and soul from bondage, snares, entanglement, diabolical entrapments and strongholds. Before you can be chosen by God as a true warrior on the frontline of battle, you must understand the power and process of deliverance.

Deliverance simply means to be totally set free from chains of spiritual bondage and demonic strongholds. Some of the chains can be spirits of poverty, hurt, pain, rejection, generational curses, ungodly soul ties and spirits of witchcraft. The power of deliverance is the peace, joy and liberty one will experience after being set free from ungodly spirits, fears and entrapments.

Deliverance for some people can be immediate however, for others, it may take a process, which may be progressive. The process of deliverance will be the pathway taken to bring you into total victory.

Deliverance empowers you with the mindset that you have the authority to choose which pathway you will take; this may mean "resetting your coordinates!"

RESETTING YOUR COORDINATES

When each one of us was born, God blessed us with a divine destiny that would bring us into success, joy, happiness, prosperity, etc. When you were born God, Himself set the coordinates of your life and programmed you so that you would be a winner. However, somewhere along your life's journey someone, something or some "things" happened to you and it altered your "coordinates."

Did you ever stop to notice how some pivotal experiences in your life altered the very course of your purpose? Looking back at them did you realize that, with all of these things happening to you, somehow your coordinates may have been shifted?

Instead of becoming a success you repeatedly experience failure; instead of going forward and progressing in life, it seems as though you are going nowhere; instead of prosperity, it seems as though you perpetually miss out attaining the blessing that God has for you.

I remember counseling a young lady who was very angry and ready to kill herself. She felt useless and could not put her hand on a single thing that she had accomplished. She felt as if she was a living, breathing puppet being controlled by something that she could not see. I realized right away that someone or something had "switched her coordinates."

Some negative experience had programmed, in her mind, that she was a failure; that she was never going anywhere and that she would never be anything in life. In other words, she needed to go through a process of deliverance.

In the case of an athlete who is on his way to becoming a "pro", he undergoes an entire regimen of reconditioning, diet modification and system detoxification. If he becomes injured at any given time, the coach immediately puts in place a plan to begin therapeutic healing.

During the past decades, there has been much debate over the concept of *"deliverance."* Many people argue that there will be no need for deliverance after accepting Jesus Christ as Lord, as His blood washes away all of our sins.

This is very true, however, throughout the Bible there are numerous accounts of people who, even after accepting Jesus, still found themselves bound by fetters, cords and ties.

> *Salvation is like entering a huge building. It is the key that gives you access. Once inside you can go into all of the other rooms. Some of these rooms include deliverance, baptism in the Holy Ghost, healings, miracles, and many others.*

In the book of Acts Ananias and Sapphira were dedicated church members but were both possessed with a lying spirit. In fact, after selling their cherished property they conspired and willfully lied about the sale price. Peter emphatically told them that they did not lie to him but lied to the Holy Ghost. Both Ananias and Sapphira paid the horrible price for this sin, which was immediate death.

Similarly, Judas was numbered among the twelve disciples but, after the Last Supper, the Bible states that satan entered him.

In another account Jesus rebuked Peter for allowing a spirit of sabotage to speak through him. Jesus never called his name; He simply addressed the demon spirit that was seeking to use Peter, who tried to prevent Him from going to the cross.

Finally, in *Mark 1:21-23* Jesus went to the synagogue where he found a man sitting, bound by an unclean spirit. Immediately Jesus rebuked the unclean spirit and restored the man's health to him.

There are countless biblical references to Jesus' encounters with demon spirits. However, it should be noted that He never ran away from them but, with compassion for the individual, He confronted the demon spirits, setting individuals totally free:

> *"...not willing that any should perish, but that all come to repentance." (2 Peter 3:9b)*

There must first be a desire for deliverance. In Matthew 15:26, Jesus refers to deliverance as the children's bread. He further stated in *John 8:36, "...whom the Son sets free is free indeed."*

Deliverance is a matter of choice. Jesus asked many people if they wanted to be made whole. In Luke 17 nine lepers were healed but only one was made whole. You have a choice in the matter. You can decide whether or not you want to be halfway free or totally free.

BREAKING THE CHAINS

Chains represent anything that would seek to keep you in bondage. Upon examining your past you would realize that at some point and time you have had chains (limiting influences) of fear, doubt, pride, and others operating in your life. Many times, the enemy uses these tactics or strategies to keep you going through painful, destructive cycles.

Chains can also represent curses, unclean spirits, obstacles, issues and great struggles. They can be developed as a result of where you live, family relationships, friendships, and even as a result of things that happened in your past. If you would examine your past, you would realize that at some point in time you have found yourself in some form of bondage and bound by chains.

These brick walls of hindrance and imprisonment have in some way, shape or form affected your progress or overall success in life.

I often hear people make comments such as: "I guess I'll never go to college", "I'm too poor to start my own business" or "I will probably pay rent forever." All of these are negative spoken words that can destroy your life. The scripture bears out that, *"Death and life are in the power of the tongue." (Proverbs 18:21)*

Therefore, you must be careful of the words that are released out of your mouth and into the atmosphere. You have the power to shape your life by the words that you speak. If many of you would be honest, you are where you are because of what you thought about yourself or because of the words that came out of your mouth.

"...as he (a man) thinketh in his heart so is he:"
(Proverbs 23:7)

In *Mark 5:1-17* the Bible speaks of a demoniac bound with chains. From time to time he would break these physical chains. However he, himself, remained bound by a spiritual condition.

Furthermore, in *Judges 16:21* Samson was bound with cords and fetters. In this account Samson had found himself in the lap of Delilah who, being used by the enemy, had sought on a number of occasions to discover the secret of his strength, a gift that was given to him by God. Compromising this anointing, Samson carelessly reveals the secret of his strength to her and later found himself bound by his enemies, with fetters of brass (chains).

In both accounts, each man was in need of deliverance. In the case of the demoniac, Jesus came in the nick of time, broke the chains over his life and made him completely whole. In the case of Samson, once his relationship with God was restored, he regained the strength to break the chains in his life. Jesus is the Anointed Chainbreaker who has declared that He has come to set the captives free. *(Luke 4:18, 19)*

Chains represent bondage and, for the most part, it takes courage to break free. Therefore, you must aggressively seek to break free from these chains and walk in power, victory and deliverance.

ISSUES, ISSUES AND MORE ISSUES

In Matthew 9:20-21 there was a woman with an issue of blood for twelve years. She knew she had an issue and was willing to get help from Jesus. Because of the constant crowd around Him, she knew that she would have to "press" in order to get to Him and eventually receive her deliverance.

Most people who are under a demonic attack know that they are, but have great struggles in getting to the person that can help them. You must fight against all odds, especially the unclean spirits that will tell you to run away from your help.

For many years I watched people come to our local church loaded with issues and curses. Upon their initial arrival they became excited especially over the prophetic words of blessing. However, I began to notice several months later when we began teaching on spiritual warfare and deliverance, many of these once excited people would begin rebelling, missing services, stirring up confusion, becoming offended by the slightest matters and, eventually, leaving the church. This greatly concerned me. Soon after, the Holy Spirit began revealing to me what was going on.

All of these people knew that there was something going on in their lives. The unclean spirits also know that if the people remained in the Church that their "days were numbered" and that they would eventually be cast out. Therefore, these spirits sought every opportunity to drive these people away from the Church.

Thus, the enemy used the spirit of offense, operating with a strong man of pride, to drive them out of the church. Whenever the Word of God is being preached, if the person is not ready to acknowledge his issues, he would reject the Word and, in a spirit of offense, build up a wall or barrier between himself and the church. In almost every case, the offended person ends up leaving the covering of the Prophet or spiritual leader through whom they can receive their deliverance.

"SKELETONS IN THE CLOSET"

If we are honest with ourselves, most of us know what "skeletons are hiding in our closets." We know the real demons that confront us every day. The demons of rage, anger, sexual or financial perversions, doubt, or low self-esteem, pride, insecurity, and even violent tendencies lurk in the cavities of our soul waiting for opportune moments to manifest and, eventually destroy us.

Further, we may be plagued by sicknesses and diseases brought on by unhealthy habits such as drinking, smoking, and sexual promiscuity. In fact, some diseases such as: sickle-cell anemia, diabetes, and hypertension or high-blood pressure, even cancer could have been inherited from the family bloodline or gene pool.

Whatever the unclean spirits are in your life, they all have a point of reference and answer to a specific name. It is imperative that you address each spirit by name and verbally command them to leave your life. You must be willing to admit to having an issue, to receive help in diagnosing the issue and state what the issue is so that the process of deliverance can begin.

STOP THE COFFIN, BREAK THE CYCLE

God has given you the power to "stop the coffin and break the cycles" in your life. The "coffin" represents everything the enemy wants to kill or cause to die in your life, be they your dreams, visions, ideas, businesses, or the literal death of people whom you cherish. You must make the decision to either let them die or break the chains and cycles of death from over your life.

The Bible gives a number of accounts of Jesus encountering situations of death, in which people were immediately brought back to life due to His divine intervention.

Firstly, on His journey, He met a Centurion who had a servant, that was about to die. Jesus spoke a word and immediately the servant was restored. *(Matthew 8:5-13)*

Jesus later interrupted a funeral where a widow from Nain's son had died and was being transported for burial. Jesus, being moved with compassion, stopped the coffin, in the midst of the procession, and broke the cycle of death, bringing him back to life.

Further, He visited Jairus' house where he met his daughter already dead. Jesus spoke two simple words to her: "Talitha Cumi", which is translated "damsel arise", and she got up. *(Mark 5:22-24, 35-43)*

245

Everyone is familiar with the story of Lazarus who had been dead for almost four (4) days, buried in a tomb with rigor mortis and decay setting in. Jesus boldly called him back to life and commanded his grave clothes to be loosed from him.

In each account Jesus intervened and was able to revive their dead situations. It does not matter if your situation is about to die, already dead and on its way to being buried, or dead and buried: regardless of whatever point of death you may find yourself at, Jesus is still the "Resurrection and the Life."

> *"...I am the Resurrection and the Life: he that believeth in me though he were dead, yet shall he live:" (John 11:25)*

Life, itself, is filled with vicious cycles. These cycles revolve through specific times and seasons and can mark crucial phases and stages in your life. Some of these cycles may be bouts of affliction, financial distress or, worst of all, death. You must get to a place where you command yourself to live and not die; you have already been anointed and empowered to do so!

IDENTIFYING CURSES

It is not the will of God to curse His children in this dispensation of grace. He desires more than anything that everyone is blessed, prosperous and living an abundant life in Him. However, if you allow your spiritual hedge of protection to be broken, you can become susceptible to the attacks of the enemy. In other words, there are some practices you may engage in which open the door to a curse coming upon your life.

These are some of the gateways and ungodly practices which may cause curses to enter your life::

- Ungodly sex (fornication, adultery, incest, bestiality, homosexuality, and the like)
- Engaging in occult practices and spiritual idolatry
- Dishonoring and disrespecting parents
- Dishonoring and disrespecting your spiritual parents (Leaders)
- Oppressing the poor and weak (abortion, neglect of the elderly, and the like)
- Generational/Ancestral Curses

"...visiting the iniquity of the fathers upon the children unto the third and fourth generation..." (Deuteronomy 5:9)

"...The fathers have eaten the sour grapes and the children's teeth are set on edge..." (Ezekiel 18:2)

GENERATIONAL/ANCESTRAL CURSES

A curse is the direct opposite of a blessing and can bring hardship, humiliation, poverty, oppression, physical and mental deficiencies. Generational or ancestral curses can be passed down from one generation to the next. Willful sins or disobedience to God's Word can open doors for curses.

Thus it is very important that you go into your family line and identify traits or hereditary issues that remain common and constant over the years and break them.

Sometimes there can be a clear indication as to the presence of curses over your life. Some examples of these indications are:

- where people are accident prone

- where there is a breakdown of marriage and family relations

- where there is chronic illnesses and sicknesses (Eg. hypertension, diabetes, sickle-cell anemia, heart disease, cancer and many others) which are repeated throughout family lineage

- where there is a history of untimely deaths or suicides

- where there is emotional, mental or schizophrenic breakdowns or disorders

- where some people operate in the spirit of extreme vagabondism (Eg., restlessness, moving from place to place, inability to settle, etc.)

- where people are constantly abused and mistreated by others

- where there are repeated, unexplainable or chronic female disorders (Eg. miscarriages, fibroids, endometriosis, and much more)

"Christ has redeemed us from the curse of the law, being made a curse for us: for it is written: 'Cursed is every one that hangeth on a 'tree." (Galatians 3:13)

If you are able to identify any of these curses in your life, you do not have to become discouraged; Jesus has already become a curse for you so that you do not have to live under these or any other curses that may seek to manifest in your life.

> *Jesus took upon Himself the form of a servant... humbled Himself and became obedient unto death even the death of the cross. (Philippians 2:7-8)*

As a believer you have kingdom rights and authority given to you by the shed blood of Jesus Christ. You can now exercise your dominion over every curse and bondage that seeks to plague your life.

GENERATIONAL BLESSINGS

Many people waste too much time focusing on generational curses. Once you have broken generational curses from over your life, you should seek to walk in your "generational blessings". God has given you the power, through the shed blood of Jesus Christ to break the powers of ancestral pacts and credence which may still be lingering over your family from previous generations. *(Galatians 3:13)*

The blessings of God are released to make you rich and add no sorrow. The Generational Blessing is irrevocable and cannot be changed. In Numbers 22, God had already blessed the children of Israel and even He could not reverse it. Balaam the prophet was overtaken by a spirit of greed and attempted to curse the children of God, but he was sharply rebuked by the Spirit of God.

"No one can curse what God has blessed!"

God has promised to bless you and your children more and more. In fact, the promise He made to Abraham in Genesis 12 to bless his seed still stands, even today.

> *"And I will make of thee a great nation, and I will bless thee, and make thy name great; and thou shalt be a blessing: And I will bless them that bless thee, and curse them that curseth thee: and in thee shall all families of the earth be blessed." (Genesis 12:2-3)*

The Bible says that Abraham was very rich in cattle, silver and gold. His son, Isaac, walked in the same blessing. This was evident as Abraham's servant went to seek out a wife for Isaac. The servant was able to give Rebekah jewels of silver, gold, and expensive clothes. Rebekah embraced the servant's offer and received a "billionaire's" generational blessing from her family.

> *"And they blessed Rebekah and said unto her, Thou art our sister, be thou the mother of thousands of millions, and let thy seed possess the gate of those which hate them."*
> *(Genesis 24:60)*

And true to this declaration, Isaac and Rebekah's seed were eternally blessed. According to *Galatians 3:19*, we are the seed of Abraham. Therefore, we must embrace our spiritual inheritance. The blessings of God are from everlasting to everlasting and His truth endureth to all generations. In **Deuteronomy 28:3, 6, 8** it declares:

> *3 Blessed shalt thou be in the city, and blessed shalt thou be in the field.*
>
> *6 Blessed shalt thou be when thou comest in, and blessed shalt thou be when thou goest out.*

⁸ The LORD shall command the blessing upon thee
in thy storehouses, and in all that thou settest thine
hand unto; and he shall bless thee in the land which
the LORD thy God giveth thee.

Begin to stake claim to every generational blessing over your life. Make prophetic declarations, calling each one upon your life and the life of your family. Blessings of health, wealth, land, houses and spiritual increase are all yours; possess them today.

Generational Blessings will come because God has promised that He would bless us with blessings and, with multiplying, multiply us. In other words, God promises to increase you more and more. God promised Abraham a generational blessing. He told him that the blessings would flow to his children and his children's children, and so shall it be unto you.

DELIVERANCE PRESCRIPTION 101
To the deliverance worker or person receiving deliverance ...

WARNING: When administering or receiving deliverance, you should first ensure that the individual seeking to be delivered is saved and has a desire to be totally set free. They must be willing to fully let go of all ungodly practices and renounce all satanic pacts, vows, covenants, all ungodly soul ties, allegiances and strongholds. Also, the individual cannot be so prideful that they are unwilling to obey the instructions of the deliverance minister.

A person undergoing deliverance may not necessarily manifest outward signs. However, if the person displays outward manifestations, this should not be taken as a sign that this person's deliverance is complete. For the most part, demons may manifest in order to distract, intimidate, deceive or cause you to lose focus. *They may even seek to bring confusion to the people that may be assisting with the deliverance by telling lies about and even threatening the deliverance worker. Demons sometimes lie about their real name so as not to be cast out. Remember that you have the authority over them; bind them and cast them out in Jesus' name.*

Additionally, if the individual is wearing demonic tattoos, symbols, jewelry, clothing or any other type of occult-related paraphernalia, these may hinder their total deliverance. In these instances where Satan's strongholds were legalized by the individual's use of any of these mechanisms, it may be necessary for you to have the item(s) removed, denounce the satanic power or the curse that it brought and have the person take back all grounds that he or she had given to the enemy.

THE PROCESS OF DELIVERANCE

In order for you to walk in your deliverance you must be willing to *acknowledge* that there is an issue in your life. Identify, assess and diagnose your true issues. You must then decide that you are now ready to be set free from the demonic strongholds tormenting your life and let them go. In order to gain your deliverance you must be willing to implement the following:

- Pray in the name of Jesus, standing in the authority of His blood
- Repent of any sin that has resulted in a curse being placed over your life – sins that you may have committed or even sins that your ancestors may have committed (which may include covenants, pacts, vows, agreements, and the like)

- Summon angelic assistance according to Psalm 103:20-22 to stand guard and warfare on your behalf
- Break all curses, including generational/ancestral curses back to the fifteenth (15th) generation or as far back as you may feel is necessary
- Denounce and break soul ties, witchcraft spells, or any other contrary or negative practices
- Bind up the strongman and the accompanying spirits; pull down demonic strongholds from operating in your life; then loose them from their diabolic assignment over your life, commanding them to go in the name of Jesus
- Close doors or plead the blood of Jesus, seal deliverance; take back grounds so that the enemy will have no legal rights to re-enter
- Release the power of God to operate in your life by declaring and activating the Word of God

As you seek to carefully follow the instructions of your physician with every medical diagnosis, you must carefully and prayerfully follow the directives of the Holy Spirit as you walk through your process of deliverance. Some of the steps in your process of deliverance may involve more emphasis being placed on a particular remedy.

For example, to effectively complete the process one individual may find days of fasting to be successful, whereas another individual may find constantly declaring the Word of God keeps them motivated and focused. Each person is different and, therefore, must seek to identify which aspect of the "prescription" works best for them.

The Word of God admonishes us in *2 Peter 1:5-8* to

[5] *"... add to your faith virtue; (moral excellence) and to virtue, knowledge; (spiritual truth)*

[6] *And to knowledge temperance; (self-control) and to temperance patience; (spiritual endurance) and to patience godliness;*

[7] *And to godliness brotherly kindness; charity, (phileo or brotherly love)*

[8] *For if these things be in you, and abound, they make you that you shall neither be barren nor unfruitful in the knowledge of our Lord Jesus Christ."*

The following are some of the physical demonstrations common to expelling certain demonic spirits that I have noticed while administering deliverance. For example someone being delivered from:

- a spirit of lust experienced burning or itching in the eyes, uncontrollable tears, or may have experience weakness or numbness in their legs
- a spirit of masturbation experienced numbness in their fingers or weakness in their knees
- a spirit of Jezebel and witchcraft experienced sensations in their hands and extreme headaches
- spirits of unforgiveness and bitterness experienced discomfort in their stomach like a tree being pulled up by the root.
- a spirit of imbalance or mental disorders may have experienced dullness, deafness or ringing in the ear

- a spirit of hurt cried profusely
- a spirit of epilepsy experienced convulsions, seizures, trembling or uncontrollable shaking
- a spirit of murder or violence may begin to "spit blood" and talk about murder or feel a desire to kill people or actually say, "I will kill you"
- a spirit of suicide may say "I want to die or I hate being alive"
- a spirit of perversion may begin gyrating, acting vulgar, flirtatious or seductive
- a spirit of profanity usually manifested using obscene language and blasphemy
- a spirit of addiction usually manifests through various behaviors depending on the nature of the addiction to food, cigarettes, cocaine, sex, television, and more. For example, for people on drugs it may be by sniffing, rubbing their nose or having an intense, deep-seated craving for their drug of choice. (This is discovered after the person receiving deliverance has been questioned.)

People may also demonstrate other reactions as demons are being expelled from them. Some of these reactions are:

- screaming
- exhaling or yawning
- coughing, spitting up or sneezing
- crawling or rolling on the floor
- shaking uncontrollably
- violent or overly aggressive behaviors (becoming destructive)
- manifesting (demonstrating) lewd behavior
- manifesting animalistic behaviors (e.g. hissing or moving like a snake, barking like a dog, acting like a monkey, charging like a bull, and more)

- grabbing or biting
- outbursts of laughter
- unusual voice changes (normally intended to intimidate you)
- distortion of facial features or expressions
- use of profanity or insults; cursing at people surrounding the deliverance worker even cursing at the deliverance worker himself

Remember, deliverance does not come by your might or your power, it comes by the Spirit of God. (Zechariah 4:6)

The 10 Commandments for Receiving and Maintaining your Deliverance and Healing

1. *Confess your sins immediately and quickly forgive others (Isaiah 59:2; Romans 6:23; Romans 10:8-10) Do not hold onto resentment or past issues. (Matthew 18:32-35)*

2. *Crucify the flesh. Do not tolerate evil thoughts or desires. You must bring your body under submission or discipline (Galatians 5:24-25; Romans 6:16)*

3. *Water Baptism (Mark 16:16)*

4. *Know that regardless of what you have done wrong, you still have the right to exercise or walk in your Spiritual Kingdom Authority (position) in Christ. (Zechariah 3:1-3)*

5. *Speak Positive Confessions, filling each empty spot now vacated by unclean spirits with the spirit of God. For example: where fear, hurt, pain and*

rejection were, release and receive the power of the love of God. Where the spirits of unbelief and doubt were, release and receive faith to operate in your life. (2 Timothy 1:7; 1 John 4:18)

6. Study and live by the Word of God, daily using scriptures to restore the affected areas in your life. His word is spirit and life (Matthew 4:4; John 6:63; Joshua 1:8; Psalm1:1-3); Man shall live by every word that proceeds out of the mouth of God.

7. Put on and keep on the Whole Armor of God every single day of your life. (Ephesians. 6:13-18) **(See more in Chapter on Spiritual Warfare)**

8. Be filled with the Holy Spirit. As you close all doors to negative past influences (people, places and things) seek to be filled with the Holy Spirit. (Ephesians 5:18) Being led by The Holy Spirit is very important to you walking in total victory.

9. Separate yourself from ungodly relations and seek Godly relationships, which includes submitting to spiritual authority (apostle, pastor) and joining yourself to a Bible-teaching church that can help you to grow and mature spiritually (Hebrews 10:24,25)

10. Plead the blood of Jesus and put on the garment of praise and worship (Isaiah 61:3)

Worship, Pray and Praise God every single minute of the day. In all things give God thanks, for this is the will of Christ Jesus [God] concerning you.

CHAPTER NINETEEN

~⊗⟨⊙⟩⊗~

THE POWER OF PREVAILING PRAYER

TONGUE POWER

"Thou shall decree a thing and it shall be established..." (Job 22:28)

Most people's lives are destroyed because of their very own tongue. The tongue is very powerful. It is referred to in the book of James as an "unruly evil." *"Death and life are in the power of the tongue:" (Proverbs 18:21).* It is very important that you understand your spiritual authority in Christ Jesus.

Constant negative remarks or negative spoken words can bring curses on your life and the lives of those around you. Words do hurt. In fact, words are so powerful that riots, civil wars, and gang fights have been started by words such as, "Go!", "Aim!", "Fire!". Words such as "Goodbye!", "Leave Now!" or "You're Fired!" have ended life-long relationships. Others such as, "I can't", "It's over!" or "I Quit!" have brought devastation to the lives of many.

259

Words are powerful. It is, therefore, important to say that many believers have given up in the midst of their walk with God because of words they have spoken or allowed others to speak over them.

Many people suffer throughout the course of their lives due to harsh, insensitive words spoken either by a parent to a child, a teacher to a student, a husband to a wife or vice versa.

Words such as, "You're stupid!", "You're Dumb!, "You'll never make it in life!", "Nobody loves you!" or "Nobody will ever marry you!", "You're ugly!", "You will always be broke!" and "You make me sick!" are just a few of the many destructive words that have been spoken and have scarred many people.

No matter how anointed or rich you are, once these negative spoken words have penetrated the core of your soul they take root and can ignite a blaze of self-destructive behavior and eventually ruin your entire life. You cannot be totally delivered or set free from these negative spoken words until you are willing to make verbal declarations to renounce what has been spoken. *(See more in Chapter 18 on The Process and Power of Deliverance)*

In the book of James it states that the tongue is an unruly member that can set on fire the whole course of nature. In other words, one word uttered from your mouth can kill or heal, stop or start, pull down or uplift, bring defeat or cause you to win. Yes, one utterance can either make or break a situation. You must now use your tongue as a weapon against the enemy to restore your life.

PRAYING IN TONGUES

"... what things soever ye desire, when you pray,
believe that ye receive them, and ye shall have them."
(Mark 11:24)

Therefore, whosoever *(no matter who you are)* if you believe without fear and doubt and ask God for whatsoever *(no matter what it is)* God is able to do it. You shall receive whatever it is that you were asking God for because your tongue has spoken it.

Further, you must be very careful of the things you speak. Many believers toss around negative words of death, thereby nullifying every promise God makes to them.

"For by thy words thou shalt be justified, and by thy words thou shalt be condemned."
(Matthew 12:37)

"Thou shalt also decree a thing and it shall be established..." (Job 22:28)

Speaking in tongues can lead you into the depths of worship, where your worship becomes warfare. However, you can limit your worship by reverting to speaking in our native tongue because your spirit man is very cognizant of your spoken words.

You cannot measure the power of speaking in tongues by what is said in the English language or your native tongue. Your heavenly language allows you greater access to navigate in the realm of the spirit as you seek to experience a greater glory of the presence of God. The spiritual ability of speaking in tongues comes upon you once you have been filled with the blessed Holy Ghost.

There are depths and realms in the Spirit that can only be attained by praying the language of the Spirit. It cannot be taught, nor inherited. You must ask the Holy Spirit to come and dwell in you and then, once you have asked, receive, by faith the Holy Spirit's infilling.

> *"... they shall speak with new tongues;"*
> *(Mark 16:17)*

> *"... out of his belly shall flow rivers of living water..."*
> *(John 7:38)*

On the day of Pentecost as one hundred and twenty believers gathered to worship and pray, the Holy Ghost descended on each of them with cloven tongues like as of fire. *(Acts 2:1-3)*

The Bible said they spoke in tongues as the Spirit gave them utterance and everyone that was around the temple heard them speaking in languages which they had never heard before. This phenomenal move of the Holy Spirit sparked a mighty Revival that led to thousands being converted in one day.

There is another level in tongue power, which is called Tongues of Angels. *(1 Corinthians 13:1)* Tongues of Angels are used to break chains in the realm of the spirit, defeating principalities and demon spirits. It is designed to break satanic interferences and activate the laws of the spirit of life in Christ Jesus.

Your deliverance at this time depends on your elevating from worship to warfare. Worship to God intercepts and breaks satanic interferences and activates the laws of the spirit of life in Christ Jesus.

As you build up your momentum during worship, spiritual angelic surveillance begins to pick up your signal on their radar. Angels that excel in strength (Psalm 103) are immediately dispatched on your behalf. The glorious victory is imminent. The Law of the Spirit of Life in Christ Jesus coupled with intense worship sets you free from all the Satanic, diabolical laws of sin and death.

MILITANT PRAYER

As your worship becomes warfare, your prayer will intensify to the point of militancy. Your militant prayer then becomes a prevailing prayer. At this point, you are now in the Z.O.N.E. This is one of the highest points in your prevailing prayer life. You become zero tolerant, not willing to compromise, make a deal or, better yet, break rank with the enemy. This is the point of no return. The spiritual missile has been launched into the realm of the spirit. It is locked into its target refusing to allow diabolical interceptions of any kind.

Many believers have spent hours, days, weeks, months, and even years in prayer, earnestly seeking answers from God, but to no avail. Sometimes frustrated and confused many of them did not realize that even though they were praying fervently, they were not praying effectively.

"... the effectual fervent prayer of a righteous man availeth much." (James 5:16b)

Your prayer must be fervent *and* effective. To advance as a sharp shooter in the realm of the spirit, you must begin to pray effective, fervent and militant prayers.

- You must see your target and focus on the specific need that warrants prayer

- Use the spirit of discernment to help you identify specific needs and how you should pray for them.
- Take your aim in the realm of the spirit, declaring God's Word, speaking specifically to the fulfillment of that need. Also, declare destruction to the enemy's plans.
- You must continuously give God thanks, glory and honor for the victory in this situation

Just as a gun is a weapon, prayer is a weapon and you cannot be afraid of prayer. You cannot be afraid to pray specific, targeted prayers that will destroy the enemy. You must know how to pray effectively and you must seek to fall in love with the weapon of prayer.

We all have access to the weapon of prayer and will discover that the more you sharpen your ability to pray, the sharper your strategies will be in spiritual warfare and spiritual intercession. There are levels of weapons as there are levels of prayer, and you must know when to use each one.

Militant Prayer will cause the target to surface. The enemy cannot stay undercover in the presence of a militant intercessor - he will be exposed. Your assignment is to shoot him down in the realm of the spirit. You have to aim precisely, speaking directly to the situation in prayer, and not miss the target.

Militant Prayer changes all circumstances and situations. It is one of the weapons used against Satan that has never lost or failed. Prayer will develop you in every area of your life. It will transform you from being a nervous and scared person to a bold saint of God. Prayer will require the right attitude and posture of worship. If you cannot worship you do not know how to pray, because prayer cultivates worship in you even as worship is a primary element of prayer.

Luke 11:1-4 outlines the model prayer, *"Our Father..."* This is a guideline on how to pray and esteem God as Father. You must acknowledge God as Father when beginning to pray. This is important because every sector, group, cult, and similar entity prays to its god. You must clearly identify and acknowledge which Lord you are praying to.

Do not spend more time thinking, worrying or fretting than seeking answers from the Spirit of God about your life. Prayer removes scales from your eyes so that you can see. It cancels spiritual blindness, uncertainty, fear and doubt.

Elijah prayed that God would open Gehazi's eyes so that he could see that there were more with them than against them. *(2 Kings 6:16-17)*

Prayer brings revelation, which is an understanding of who you are and who is with you. In *Psalm 23* David confidently says, *"...Thou art with me..."*.

"Thou" here represents God, and He is the epitome of everything you need. It is He that will go with you to work, the bank, the grocery store and everywhere you go. It is God who is working to bring you the victory in every area of your life. His rod and staff also go with you. The rod is used for guidance and to do the miraculous, whereas the staff is used for protection and is designed to keep you out of harmful situations. The Holy Ghost is your rod and staff; angels accompany you. You have to dwell in God (Psalm 91) and be a walking *"prayer bomb"* everywhere you go!

PREVAILING PRAYER

"And there was war in heaven: Michael and his angels fought against the dragon; and the dragon fought and his angels, and prevailed not;..." (Revelation 12:7-8)

As stated above, Michael, the Archangel of God, skillfully fought against satan and he (satan) lost. When you pray strategic warfare prayers involving angelic assistance, the victory is always guaranteed. When we pray, God immediately releases answers.

Some of those prevailing prayers that will give you guaranteed results are listed below. However, more details about them are in the book by author entitled, *"The Power Of Yokebreaking Prayers"*

Other prevailing prayers include, but are not limited to:
- Vertical Prayers
- Praying in the Holy Spirit
- Prayer of Intoxication
- Prayers of Petition
- Prayers of Lamentation
- Prayers of Supplication
- Prayers of Faith
- Prayers of Thanksgiving
- Prayers of Repentance
- Prayers of Consecration
- Intercessory Prayers
- Warfare Prayers
- Prophetic Prayers
- Prayers of Agreement
- Persistent Prayers

You have been mandated by God to pray without ceasing *(1 Thessalonians 5:17)* and prevail (that is, to win). Do not doubt when you pray. When we pray, God immediately releases our answers *(1 John 5:14).*

Many people spend most of their time praying horizontally, distracted by demonic interferences. God, however, expects us to pray heaven-bound, vertical prayers.

These prayers go straight to the throne room of God like a spiritual rocket, creating portals and prompting immediate responses from the hand of God. Most people give up on the verge of their breakthrough. You must persevere.

In *Genesis 32:28* Jacob had this exact experience. After his dream of angels ascending and descending he wrestled with an angel until the breaking of day and prevailed. Not only was his name changed from deceiver to Israel, but he was immediately "up-ranked" in the realm of the spirit as a prince who now had spiritual authority in heaven and on earth. *Prevailing prayer pulls down strongholds:*

> *" For the weapons of our warfare are not carnal, but they are mighty through God to the pulling down of strongholds; Casting down imaginations and every high thing that exalteth itself against the knowledge of God,..." (2 Corinthians 10:4-6)*

Prevailing prayer is able to reach within you, pulling down strongholds and trampling on imaginations. It is very powerful and able to reach "every high thing" in your life. These "every high things" can be thoughts of doubt, fear, suicide, insecurities, anxieties, worries, other mind battles or any other thing that seeks to exalt itself against the knowledge or anointing of God in your life.

This powerful weapon of prevailing militant prayer will cast down and trample every plan of the enemy, bringing into captivity every thought to the obedience of Christ.

"Against" denotes a fighting word; it is anything trying to oppose or contradict who God already said you are. For example, you may think that you are poor but God's Word declares that you are rich. You may feel sick, but God's Word says, "You are healed!" You may feel lonely, but God's Word says that He will never leave you nor forsake you.

You may be confused, but the Word of God says that you have peace. You may be fearful, but God's Word says that His love has cast out all fear in your life. In actuality, when you pray this type of prayer, you are literally destroying the enemy's false infiltrations into your mind.

Supplication and *Lamenting Prayer* are acts of pouring out one's self; to be broken; to break your alabaster box at the feet of Jesus like Mary did; to cry out to God like Hannah did in *1 Samuel 3:1*. This leads to a prayer of intoxication or drunkenness; after intoxication is the climax - the release or the place where God will speak to you – and change your entire situation.

Daniel demonstrated persistent prayer. He prayed for twenty-one (21) days and gained access into the throne room of God and received angelic assistance. When you pray, you will experience angelic visitation. Your persistent prayer (Luke 18:1-8) will bring you into prevailing prayer. Consistent prayer is praying without ceasing.

Travailing in prayer - When Zion travails, she brings forth sons and daughters. You give birth to your dreams, visions and ideas when you travail and prevail in prayer *(Isaiah 66:7-8)*. When you begin to pray travailing prayers, your physical eyes may be closed, but your spiritual eyes will be opened. According to *Ephesians 1:18* your spiritual discernment will become more accurate when you pray. Through your prayers you are enlightened to the things of God.

BINDING THE SPIRITS OF BACKLASH & RETALIATION
Beware of the Siamese Twins

It is very important that you continue in your attitude of worship, prayer and warfare because most people, after a glorious victory, go to sleep and take a vacation. "Brutish", petty demons full of resentment and fury known as the "hit and run" twins - "backlash and retaliation" - always get angry and attack immediately after spiritual victories.

They often return loaded with a vengeance of offense, false accusations, lies, infirmity, affliction, pain, suicide, confusion, frustration, accidents and incidences, worst of all, invoking feelings of worthlessness and despair in their victims. (1 King 19:1-5) If you are not prepared or aware, their subliminal detrimental blow can knock you totally off of your feet.

These demon spirits seldom attack when you are spiritually conscious. For the most part, they wait until you are most vulnerable. For example, after you have left church and had a mighty move of God, after you have just received a prophetic word, after you have sown seeds, ministered the word in dance, song or preached, these demonic spirits launch their attack.

The most effective weapons against "Backlash and Retaliation" are exposure and cancellation of their diabolical assignments before they can manifest.

"But speak thou the things which become sound doctrine." (Titus 2:1)

Strive not to speak or pray erroneous, foolish words that will send negative signals, attracting unwanted problems to your life. Many people say foolish things to Satan such as, "I am going to kill you" - these words only generate frustration in the demonic realm and attract unwanted problems and demonic spirits to your life.

God desires to release so much of His power and anointing upon us, but how much are we able to sustain? Our capacity to hold and carry His glory will be determined based upon the volume of space we create while worshipping. The more we pour out in our worship, the more we can demand.

In *2 Kings 4:1-7*, the more vessels the widow woman had, the more oil flowed, enabling her to pay her debts. When she ran out of vessels the oil stopped flowing. The anointing works almost the same way. The more time we spend available worshipping and praying, the more anointing oil the Father will pour out upon us to remove burdens and destroy yokes. The more yokes we destroy, the more glory goes to God our Father through our life.

It is only when we cease to worship and seek the face of God that the oil of the anointing stagnates and we do not experience the level of blessing and power to which we are entitled. Continue stirring up the anointing on your life and doing God's work, you will experience volumes of glory, which cannot be contained.

CHAPTER TWENTY

ANOINTED TO RULE AND REIGN

WALKING IN THE ANOINTING

"Anointed" is a popular word tossed around in Christian circles as the qualifier of the "who's who" and "what's what" in the Church. However, very few people really understand its TRUE meaning.

To anoint is to "smear on all over" (that is, to be totally immersed and entrenched). It is the outpouring of oil from the top of the head running down to the end of your garments. As in *Psalm 133:2*, the Bible speaks about how the anointing runs down Aaron's head unto his beard, down to his skirt.

The purpose of the anointing is to remove burdens and destroy yokes in every area of our lives and in the lives of those around us.   David said, *"... thou anointest my head with oil, my cup runneth over." (Psalm 23:5b)* In other words, he became so entrenched in the presence of God that it overflowed in every area of his life.

His first anointing encounter was at the young age of about sixteen years.   David had been busy in his father, Jessie's field minding and protecting his father's sheep when the prophet Samuel came to anoint one of Jessie's sons as the next king of Israel.   David, although the youngest of his siblings, was chosen by God as "the one", the next anointed King of Israel.

Samuel brought with him a horn of oil. Symbolically pouring the oil upon David's head, Samuel announced that he would be the next king over all Israel. The following day David resumed his duties in his father's field.

Anointing with oil was a common practice among the Jews.   However, the Kings, Priests and Prophets were ceremonially anointed as they took on the responsibilities of these offices.

The accounts of David's experiences, as a youth being attacked by the lion and the bear and defeating them both, are what I call *"anointed."*   Goliath was his next challenge - David also defeated him. Every situation David encountered released more levels of the anointing on his life to perform the next assignment. Almost fifteen years later he mounted his royal throne. From the day of his anointing he began to rule and reign. The day he sat on the throne was the day they called him king.

Similarly, as Aaron was anointed as a priest in *Leviticus 8:12* it was poured all over his head and ran down his beard, even to the skirts of his garments. In *Psalm 133:2* it says how fellowship is like the precious ointment upon the head that ran down upon the beard, even Aaron's beard, that went down to the skirts of his garments.

God expects us, as his kings and priests, to become so soaked in His glory that we subdue kingdoms and dominate every single area around us. Jesus said in *Luke 4:18:*

> *"The spirit of the Lord is upon Me, because He*
> *(the Lord) hath anointed Me to preach the*
> *gospel to the poor; He hath sent me to heal the*
> *broken-hearted to preach deliverance to the*
> *captives, and recovering of sight to the blind,*
> *to set at liberty them that are bruised."*

ANOINTED TO RULE AND REIGN

We must understand that the anointing comes upon our lives to do something for God that we are not able to do in our own strength. We must begin to operate in the anointing (God-breathed, God-inspired gifts, talents and abilities) that has been given to us. Taking it (everything that God has blessed us with) to the grave is a waste; ruling and reigning with it is a must!

It is so important that we aggressively seek to fulfill God's mandate. The anointing on our lives equips us for everything God is calling us to do. Much too often believers wait until they are physically seated in a position before they begin to function. God has already anointed us by his precious Holy Spirit to walk in our divine, God-appointed assignment.

We must begin slaying bears, lions and giants before we get to *"the seated place."* Your acceptance of Jesus as Lord and Savior entitles you to this empowerment. Paul said that we are seated with God in heavenly places, far above all principalities *(Ephesians 2:6).* To be "seated with Christ" is a place of spiritual authority and position.

Jesus died, paid the price for us, went back to heaven and sat down beside His Father. His blood gives us legal access so that whatsoever we bind on earth is bound in heaven and whatsoever we loose on earth is loosed in heaven. *(Matthew 18:18)* You do not need to be ordained as a prophet, priest, or pope before you start slaying giants.

God has uniquely anointed each of us with a "more than a conqueror" ability to eradicate every plot, plan and strategy of Satan. Behold, now God has given you power (Gk – exousia; *pronounced ex-oo-see'-ah*) and authority over all the powers or abilities of the enemy, and *"...nothing shall by any means hurt you." (Luke 10:19)* Because of your Kingdom Ambassadorship, even though at times the enemy may *"bruise your heel,"* you have been anointed by God to *"bruise his head" (Genesis 3:15).*

KINGDOM AMBASSADORSHIP

"...The kingdoms of this world are become the kingdoms of our Lord, and of His Christ; and He shall reign for ever and ever.
(Revelations 11:15)

God, through His sovereignty has set up His kingdom as a powerful dimension. This dimension can only be accessed through one's spiritual perception and conception. Once we accept Jesus Christ as Lord and personal savior, God allows man to govern and have authority in this realm. This spiritual realm is, therefore, our domain and each one of us has been given dominion as a king to be fruitful, multiply, replenish, subdue and dominate in it on earth. (Revelations 1:6, Genesis 1:28)

The Kingdom of heaven is not a particular denominational label, a long white dress or a short black one. Rather, it is our mindset, the way we perceive things and, most of all, it is the way we live.

As a Kingdom Ambassador, it is very important to remember that even though you live on earth, you represent a totally different Kingdom that demonstrates healing, deliverance, prosperity, loyalty, royalty, creativity, wealth, diplomacy, empowerment and holiness. This kingdom has its own spiritual ideologies, laws, concepts and much more.

*¹⁰ Thy kingdom come, Thy will be done in
earth, as it is in heaven. (Matthew 6:10)*

You must see your kingdom ambassadorship solely as revolutionary in nature with a mission to affect, infect and bring spiritual or positive change to this present world order, as you must begin to see yourself as apostolic and prophetic ambassadors for Christ. *(Ephesians 4:11)* Your ambassadorial anointing affords you the privilege of being in this world but not conformed to this world system. *(Romans 12:2)*

In addition, *Matthew 5:14* says we are the light of the world. Your anointed, "blood stamped" passport gives you diplomatic immunity to every evil conspiracy, sickness, disease or weaponry that may be formed against you. Know that "they shall not prosper."

You have been given total liberty to manifest the kingdom of God (that is, all the excellencies of God revealed). Therefore, gird up your loins, take out your keys and begin operating in your divine kingdom authority today.

*"...For thine is the kingdom, and the power,
and the glory for ever Amen." (Matthew 6:13)*

As a warrior called to the frontline of battle you must understand your rank, position and job description. The Word of God reveals that *"we are seated with Christ in heavenly places." (Ephesians 1:3; Ephesians 2:6).*

In other words, you are already in a place of spiritual authority because of the blood of Jesus and you are a joint heir with Christ. I declare to you today that you already have the power in Jesus' name.

THE DIVINE PLAN OF GOD
God Has A Divine Purpose And Calling For Your Life

- ❖ *Your divine appointment (kairos – your God-ordained moment) brings you to your divine purpose*
- ❖ *Your divine purpose gives you a divine assignment*
- ❖ *Your divine assignment ignites a divine impartation*
- ❖ *Your divine impartation inspires divine revelations*
- ❖ *Your divine revelations release divine manifestations*
- ❖ *Your divine manifestations forge divine connections*
- ❖ *Your divine connections point you to your divine destiny.*

Many people go through life in search of their purpose. They are uncertain as to who they are, why they are here and, worst of all, where they are going.

Purpose can be defined as the original intent for which something has been created. For example, a chair was created to sit in, a bed to sleep on and a bucket to hold water. Whereas these are not the only things that they can do, it was one of the original intents for which they were designed. Therefore you, as an individual, must seek the face of God in search of why you were created.

When God called your name, there was some void in the earth realm that God wanted filled. Each one of us was birthed with a God-given assignment and purpose. Thus, as you go before God, seek to know what His divine will is in your life.

Walking in your divine purpose in the kingdom may, at first, seem confusing, frustrating and uncomfortable. However, as you continue to work or to enhance what it is God has assigned you to do, you will find that it becomes more and more satisfying and gratifying each day. Whenever you are operating in your divine purpose, you will experience a peace which passes all understanding.

FULFILLING GOD'S PURPOSE IN YOUR LIFE

The more we are available to God

The more space He takes up in our lives!

The greater the capacity, the more we increase.

The greater we increase, the greater the volume.

The greater the volume, the more the demand.

The greater the demand, the more the supply.

The more we are able to supply,

the more God pours into us.

Do not become distracted while in pursuit or in search of your divine purpose and kingdom assignment. To live a life without purpose is to merely exist. Seek to do more than just exist. You have the potential to accomplish great things for God.

SPIRITUAL POTENTIAL

Potential is your ability to do something. Some Christians are not maximizing their fullest potential, but are only operating on a fraction of their abilities and capabilities. This is not God's original intent for man. He created man to have dominion – to rule over.

In order to have dominion you must be operating in or walking with potential and power. Before the fall of man, man operated in supreme potential and purpose. God placed Adam in the garden and gave him dominion and authority. In *Genesis 2:20*, Adam was able to name all the cattle of the field, the fowl of the air and beast of the field because he was walking in his God-given potential.

Einstein was one of the smartest men to walk the face of the earth. He created formulas, laws, and theories that are still operational and in practice today. However, he only used a small fraction (less than one-third) of his brain's potential. Can you imagine what the results could have been, if he operated in one hundred percent of his potential ability?

God is saying to you today that it is time for you to use your spiritual abilities and spiritual potential. God has given you supernatural power to "decree and declare" and "to rule and to reign."

YOUR KINGDOM SPIRITUAL AUTHORITY

One of the things I have noticed over the years is that not many spiritual soldiers understand their authority. One of satan's biggest weapons of mass destruction against the body of Christ is "ignorance." Paul, a man accustomed to waging war against the saints before his conversion, reminds believers after being converted that *"...we are not ignorant of his satan's) devices ..." (2 Corinthians 2:11)*.

Your divine kingdom authority is given to you by God and qualifies you to have whatsoever you say. Laws and principles govern the kingdom. You may live your life moving from level to level, but you will only become established on dimensions.

A dimension encompasses a realm of established higher thought that will govern how you live. This realm of higher thoughts, once realized, is called a paradigm. When you begin to move in the direction and follow the directives of those thoughts, you experience what is called a *paradigm shift*. This shifting changes the atmosphere. Once the atmosphere is changed, a new climate is created.

Depending on what the climate is, it will stimulate a new culture. This culture will depict the way you speak, the way you live, your fashion trends and the way you perceive things. You must walk away from former social systems and become acclimated to your new environment.

Your abilities, through worship and warfare, help to cultivate new paradigms. This empowerment will help you to pull down negative strongholds, changing the way you think, the songs you listen to, the books you read and the desires you have. Once these strongholds have been destroyed, you would have developed new habits. The development of these new habits, if maintained, will produce a new culture. This new culture creates a new mindset and, eventually, a brand new lifestyle.

God wants us to be spiritual thermostats, setting the climate, causing others to follow. The thermometer on the other hand, changes to suit the climate. We, through consistent worship, will influence entire kingdoms, domains and nations.

JUST A.S.K. (ASK, SEEK AND KNOCK)

In Matthew 7:7 Jesus gives us an easy three-step plan for breaking chains and walking in power. He said,

"ASK" and it shall be given (a guaranteed result is imminent when your tongue and vocal cords are engaged).

"SEEK"- and you shall find (to search diligently, seeing only your victorious outcome)

"KNOCK" - and the door shall be opened unto you (persistently, continuously, praying with all boldness and confidence knowing that the doors of opportunity and blessings have already been opened unto you.)

SWEATLESS VICTORIES

Even though the war we are engaged in is a ceaseless one, there comes a time in every soldier's life when he becomes weary of fighting. This is not a sign of weakness but it should be viewed as a season and a time of rest.

[1]"To everything there is a season, and a time to every purpose under the heaven;

[7]A time to rend, and a time to sew; a time to keep silence, and a time to speak;

*⁸A time to love and a time to hate; a time of
war and a time of peace."
(Ecclesiastes 3:1, 7, 8)*

There is a set time in God when you have a *"kairos
moment"* or an opportune moment. It is now used in
theology to describe the qualitative form of time. This
moment is a God-ordained appointed time where there is no
need to fight or be afraid because your victory is sure. At this
level you know that God has heard you, and that it is just a
matter of time until your breakthrough manifests.

Can you imagine having to fight every single second of
your day without rest? You will be worn out, fatigued and
frustrated. This is not God's will for your life. Jesus reminds
us in *John 10:10* that He came that we might have life and
have it more abundantly. His desire is for us to prosper as a
direct result of the well-being and prosperity of our soul
(mind, will, intellect and emotions).

After a lifetime of spiritual warfare, prayer and
worship, you attain to a point of spiritual maturity. At this
point you come into a full understanding of your legal rights
as a believer. It is during this time in your life that God gives
you what are called "sweatless victories." As an anointed
warrior and king, David had many days of such victories.

However, one of the most memorable victories
recorded in the Bible occurred in the military career of King
Jehoshaphat . *(2 Chronicles 20:15–23)* In this account, after
the children of God had assumed the battle position of
worship, God sent invisible ambushments in the midst of the
enemy and caused them to defeat themselves.

When you have gone through seasons in your life and your worship takes you beyond warfare there is no need to fight; your faith qualifies your victory. Sweatless victories are benefits of your kingdom ambassadorship."

WAITING TO EXHALE

It is amazing that so many people go through life holding their breath, waiting to exhale. We live in a world where, effortlessly, every second we are able to breathe in and out without even having to think about it. Although this is a physical or rather, natural phenomenon to keep our life systems functioning, it is amazing how so many people still feel as though they are suffocating due to the many pressures and stresses of life.

You are probably one such person. If the truth were told, behind your beautiful face and painted smile there is someone who is frustrated over life's daily issues and you are just waiting to exhale.

In *Genesis 2:7*, God did a great thing when He created Adam, but when He breathed (*nshamah* – the Hebrew word for 'wind'; *pronounced nesh-aw-naw*) His breath or Himself into Adam to me, that was more powerful than anything that took place in Eden that day. What God released into Adam was the *"zoe"* life. Zoe is a Greek word (pronounced dzo-ay).

Further, it was a dimension of spiritual authority that allowed him to dominate not merely a small "Edenic" region, but an entire domain, activating God's divine will on earth, even as it was being done in heaven. Whatever Adam called the animals, to this very day, that is exactly what they are. To this day, all are functioning and operating within their divine purpose.

Like Israel, in Ezekiel chapter 37, you may feel somewhat scattered; everywhere seemingly void of God or His presence. As you prophesy upon the dry bones, so shall all the pieces in your life including your family, business, ministry, community and nation come back together again.

After going through the dimensions from worship to warfare you have been empowered to live and God is simply waiting on you to exhale. Just like the dry bones in Ezekiel, you are now feeling your bones coming together and could almost stand on your own two feet. You may even feel a little stronger than you did yesterday, but somehow there still seems to be something missing out of you. *Do not give up!*

The bones all received sinews (salvation), flesh (the form of godliness), skin (spoke in tongues), but still had no breath (no life or anointing power). Ezekiel was mandated to prophecy (*na'ba*) to the four winds (*ru'wach*-Hebrew) and commanded the breath (*ru'wach*-Hebrew) to come upon them. In verse ten (10), the breath finally came; they began to live again and stood upon their feet as an exceeding great army.

Many people in the body of Christ are in a similar "valley of dry bones" and, like the children of Israel, may be experiencing spiritual dryness. For others it may be dryness in their finances, in their jobs, in their businesses, in their marriages, or other personal areas in their lives. Do not stay dry. Do not die. Stand up on your feet and begin to blow or prophesy and command your situations to change in Jesus' name.

For you, it may appear that no matter how hard you try, things just do not seem to be getting any better. This is now your season and your time in God. You have been given the same privilege as Adam to shape your "Eden" and change your destiny. Open wide now your mouth and, with a forceful gush of wind, *Exhale (ie., prophesy or declare)*.

> *"Breathing in fills your lungs with air, just as breathing out (exhaling), fills your world with life. Know that you now have the power to shape your world by your words."*

God has brought you out of bondage and has broken every chain, cord, fetter and tie from over your life. He has put all of Him in you. Keep not silent; jump up on your feet, open your mouth again and let him fill it as you breathe on everything around you that is simply *"Waiting for you to Exhale"*.

> *"I am the Lord your God, Who bought you up out of the land of Egypt. Open your mouth wide and I will fill it." (Ps. 81:10)*

THE RETURN OF THE ARK

The earth is about to "ring again" because the glory of God is coming back to your life. In *1 Samuel 4:5*, the Philistines defeated the children of Israel. The bible says that they wept before the Lord and brought the Ark of the Covenant back out of Shiloh. When the Ark (which represents the presence of God) came out of Shiloh in their midst, they shouted and the earth "rang" again so that their enemies became very afraid. Revival returned to the camp of Israel.

The entire earth is about to "ring" again. It is about to shake. The earth is about to experience you and your God because His glory has now come back upon your life and shall come back to the Nations.

INDEX

THE CRY OF THE NATIONS...

Teach us to worship
Teach us to praise
Teach us God's Word
And Teach us His Ways

Teach us to go in
And possess the land
Teach us to conquer
And teach us to stand

Teach us to fast
To Overcome sin
Teach us spiritual warfare
Teach us to win

Teach us to love
Teach us to live
Teach us humility
And how to forgive

Teach us to serve
And give our best
Teach us, O Mighty Warrior
How to pass the test!

Psalm 22:27-28

All the ends (nations) of the world shall remember and turn unto the Lord: and all the kindreds of the nations (the whole earth) shall worship before thee." (v27)

For the kingdom is the Lord's: and He is the governor among the nations. (v28)

286

Prophetess Dr. Mattie Nottage BA, MA, DD

MINISTRY PROFILE

Widely endorsed as a prophet to the nations, God has used Dr. Mattie Nottage to captivate audiences around the world through her insightful, life-changing messages.

Dr. Nottage is married to Apostle Edison Nottage. She co-pastors, along with her husband, Believers Faith Outreach Ministries, International in Nassau, Bahamas.

Mantled with an uncanny spirit of discernment and an undeniable prophetic anointing, Dr. Nottage is a well-respected international preacher, prolific teacher, motivational speaker, life coach, playwright, author, gospel recording artist and revivalist.

She is the President and Founder of *Mattie Nottage Ministries, International, The Global Dominion Network Empowering Group of Companies, The Youth In Action Group and The Faith Village For Girls Transformation Program. She is also The Chancellor of The Mattie Nottage School of Ministry. She is the Founder of the prestigious Mattie Nottage Outstanding Kingdom Woman's Award.*

Dr. Nottage has ministered the gospel, in places such as: Ireland, Brazil, Africa, The Netherlands, throughout the United States of America and The Caribbean. Gifted with an authentic anointing, God uses her to "set the captive free" and to fan the flames of revival throughout the nations. Dr. Mattie Nottage, has an endearing passion to train and equip individuals to advance the Kingdom of God and walk in total victory.

She is the author of her bestselling book, *"Breaking The Chains, From Worship to Warfare", "Secrets Every*

*Mother Should Tell Her Daughter About Life" Book &
Journal* and her newly released book *"I Refuse To Die!* Dr.
Nottage is also a regular columnist in The Tribune, the
national newspaper of the Bahamas. She has also written
numerous publications, stage plays and songs, including the
#1 smash hit CD Singles, *"The Verdict Is In...Not Guilty!"*
and *"I Still Want You!"*

She has regularly appeared as a guest on various
television networks including The Trinity Broadcasting
Network (TBN), The Word Network, The Atlanta Live TV
and The Babbie Mason Talk Show "Babbie's House" amongst
others. Additionally, Dr. Mattie Nottage has been featured in
several magazine publications such as the Preaching Woman
Magazine and the "Gospel Today" Magazine as one of
America's most influential pastors. She, along with her
husband, Apostle Edison are the hosts of their very own
television show, "Transforming Lives" which airs weekly on
The Impact Network.

Dr. Nottage is the former Chairman of the National
Youth Advisory Council to the government of the Bahamas
and was also recognized and awarded a *"Proclamation of
State" by the Mayor and Commissioner of Miami-Dade County,
Florida* for her exemplary community initiatives that bring
transformation and empowerment to the lives of youth and
families globally.

Further, Dr. Nottage has earned her, Bachelor of Arts
degree in Christian Counseling, a Masters of Arts degree in
Christian Education, and a Doctor of Divinity degree from the
renown St. Thomas University, in Jacksonville, Florida and is
also a graduate of Kingdom University. Additionally, she has
earned her Certified Life Coaching Degree from the F. W. I.
Life Coach Training Institute.

Dr. Mattie Nottage is known as a Trailblazer and a
"Doctor of Deliverance" who is committed and dedicated to
Breaking Chains and Transforming Lives!

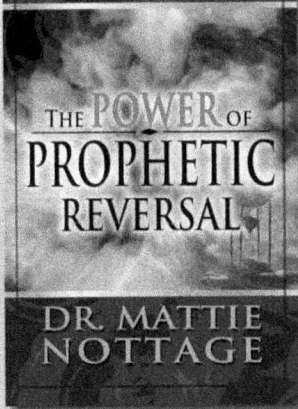

ORDER YOUR COPY NOW!!

...ne weapons of our warfare are not carnal, but are mighty through God..." (2 Cor. 10:4)

Breaking THE CHAINS
FROM WORSHIP TO WARFARE
"SURVIVING THE CONFLICT"
E NOTTAGE

"A Power-Packed Book for Women & Girls!"
Secrets EVERY MOTHER Should Tell Her DAUGHTER ABOUT Life
DR. MATTIE NOTTAGE

Secrets "... As I Navigate Through This Thing Called Life!"
Secrets EVERY MOTHER Should Tell Her DAUGHTER ABOUT Life JOURNAL
Dr. Mattie Nottage

Breaking The Chains -From Worship to Warfare

Secrets Every Mother Should Tell Her Daughter About Life
BOOK & JOURNAL

MATTIE
NOTTAGE
I STILL
WANT YOU
HIT CD SINGLE
Get Your
Copy Now!
MATTIE
NOTTAGE
I STILL
WANT YOU
Coming Soon!
I STILL WANT YOU - THE BOOK
Tel: (242) 698-1383 or (888) 825-7568
www.mattienottage.org
FOLLOW US ON

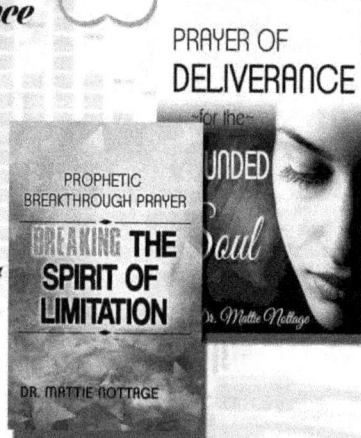

To request Dr. Mattie Nottage for a speaking engagement, upcoming event, life coaching seminar or mentorship session or to place an order for products, please contact:

Mattie Nottage Ministries, International (Bahamas Address)
P.O. Box SB-52524
Nassau, N. P. Bahamas
Tel/Fax: (242) 698-1383 or
(954) 237-8196

OR

Mattie Nottage Ministries, International (U.S. Address)
6511 Nova Dr., Suite #193
Davie, Florida 33317

Tel/Fax: **(888) 825-7568**
UK Tel: 44 (0) 203371 9922

OR

www.mattienottage.org

Follow us on:
Facebook @ DrMattie Nottage
and Twitter 🐦 @ DrMattieNottage

www.ingramcontent.com/pod-product-compliance
Lightning Source LLC
Chambersburg PA
CBHW060004100426
42740CB00010B/1395